Larry James Smith

GOOFY presents
The Olympics
**A Fun and Exciting History of the Olympics
From the Ancient Games to Today**

BOOK CLUB EDITION

GOOFY presents

The Olympics

**A Fun and Exciting History of the Olympics
From the Ancient Games to Today**

Photograph Credits: Alpha Photo Associates, Inc./J. Zimmerman, 50 (top); The American Numismatic Society, 15; The Bettmann Archive Inc., 12, 18; Brown Brothers, 24; Jerry Cooke/SPORTS ILLUSTRATED, 34, 41, 43, 44, 45 (top), 47, 54 (top), 55, 78, 87, 88, 90, 103, 106; Culver Pictures, Inc., 20; James Drake/SPORTS ILLUSTRATED, 52, 74, 88 (inset), 98, 102, 108 (right); Helmut Gritscher/SPORTS ILLUSTRATED, 30; Walter Iooss Jr./SPORTS ILLUSTRATED, 64, 65, 81 (top), 82 (top), 86, 93; Keystone Press Agency, Inc., 25; Heinz Kluetmeier/SPORTS ILLUSTRATED, 26, 33, 73, 75, 81 (bottom), 83, 84; Neil Leifer/SPORTS ILLUSTRATED, cover, 37 (top), 38, 39, 42, 48, 62, 63, 67, 77, 91, 95, 97, 99, 108 (left); Flip Schulke/SPORTS ILLUSTRATED, 92; Eric Schweikardt/SPORTS ILLUSTRATED, 101, 109; T. Tanuma/SPORTS ILLUSTRATED, 40; Tony Triolo/SPORTS ILLUSTRATED, 45 (bottom), 50 (bottom), 54 (bottom and right), 57, 96, 104, 110; United Press International, 36, 51, 58, 66, 70; Wide World Photos, Inc., 49, 60, 61, 69, 82 (bottom); John G. Zimmerman/SPORTS ILLUSTRATED, 37.

Copyright © 1979 by Walt Disney Productions. All rights reserved under International and Pan-American Copyright Conventions. Published in the United States by Random House, Inc., New York, and simultaneously in Canada by Random House of Canada Limited, Toronto.
Library of Congress Cataloging in Publication Data
Disney (Walt) Productions.
  Goofy presents the Olympics.
  Includes index.
  SUMMARY: Presents a brief history of the ancient and modern Olympic games.
  1. Olympic games—History—Juvenile literature.
[1. Olympic games—History] I. Title.
GV721.5.D55   1979   796.4'8'09   79-18177
ISBN 0-394-84224-3 (trade)   ISBN 0-394-94224-8 (lib. bdg.)
Manufactured in the United States of America   1 2 3 4 5 6 7 8 9 0
A B C D E F G H I J K

Introduction

Every four years, people from all around the globe come together to compete in the most important and exciting events held for amateur athletes—the Olympics!

Athletes in every country train endless hours and compete in countless contests for the honor of representing their country in the Olympics. The contestants—men and women, young and old—work toward their greatest goal, to win an Olympic gold medal.

On the following pages you will find the story of the Olympic games: how they started, the great traditions that have been passed down through the years, and some of the heroic performers who have brought glory to themselves and their countries.

Contents

1. The Ancient Olympic Games — 13
2. The Modern Olympics — 21
3. Olympic Preparations — 27
4. The Opening Olympic Ceremony — 31
5. The Winter Olympics — 35
6. The Summer Olympics — 53
7. The Closing Olympic Ceremony — 107
   Index — 111

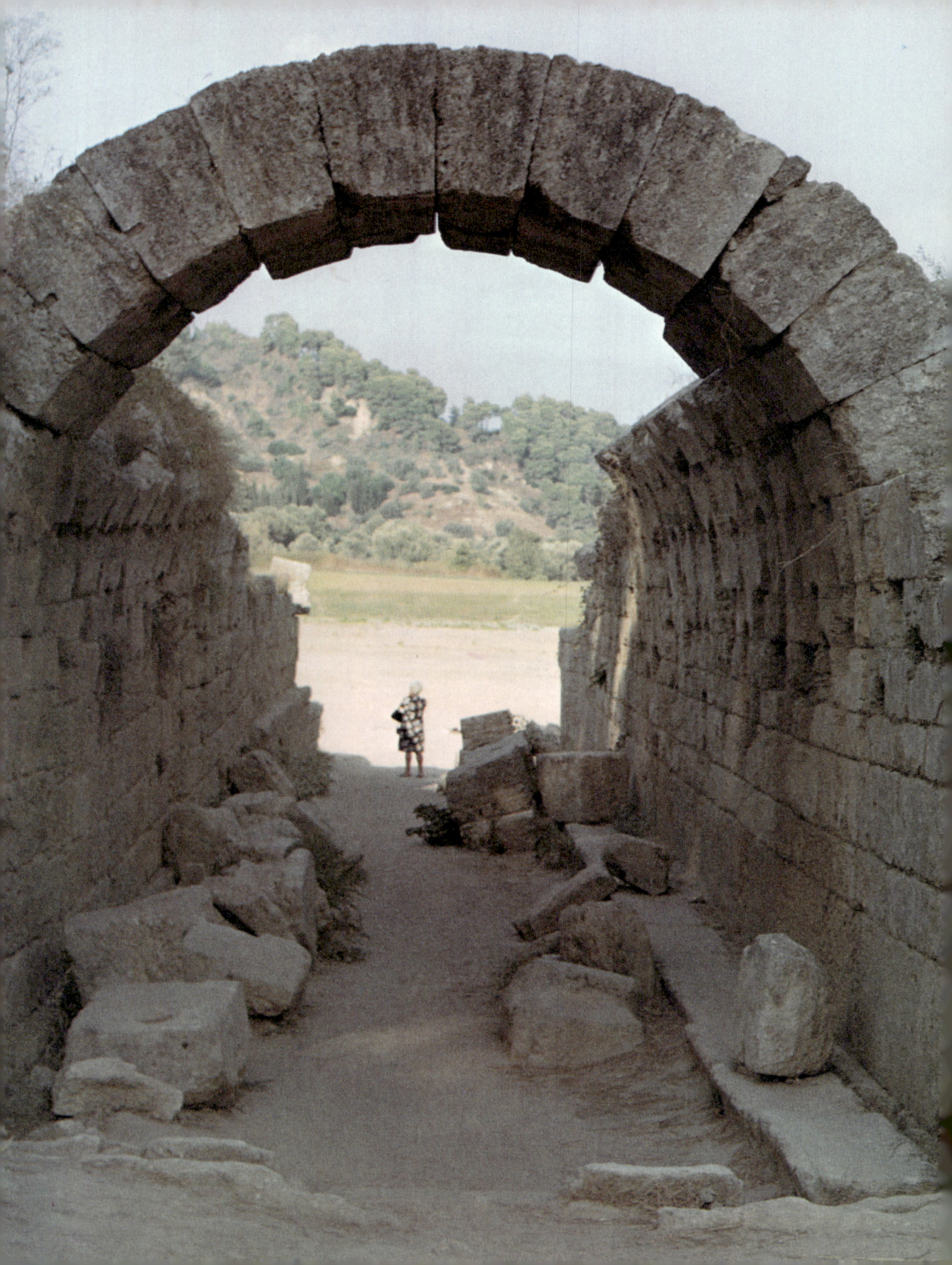

1

The Ancient Olympic Games

We know that the ancient Olympic games were held every 4 years for more than 1,000 years in the Olympia Valley of Greece. We don't know for sure how, why, or when they were started. One of the legends about the Olympics, passed down through the years, concerned a wonderously strong man, Herakles (HER-uh-kleez). We know him better by his Roman name—Hercules (HUR-cue-leez).

According to the story, the gods ordered Herakles to clean out the huge stables of Augeas (awe-GEE-us), king of Elis, a city in Greece. The stables had not been cleaned in a year, and poor Herakles had to finish this huge task in just a single day. It was an impossible job for any ordinary man. But Herakles was not ordinary. He had extraordinary strength. He could fight a lion with his bare hands!

Using his power, Herakles changed the direction of two rivers so that they flowed right through the stables. The water cleaned the stables! Herakles was so grateful to have finished the job on time that it is said he began the games in Zeus's honor. Zeus was the most important god of all the gods and goddesses that the Greeks worshiped.

In that ancient time, the cities in Greece were always fighting with each other for one reason or another. Two cities, called Pisa and Elis, went to war because each one claimed to have

Gateway to stadium at Olympia, Greece

13

thought up the idea of the athletic games in the Olympia valley. In 884 B.C. a truce was called so that the contests could be held in peace. The truce was in effect during the time the games were played. That meant that anyone in Greece who wanted to watch or compete in the games could travel safely to the Olympia valley.

The peace treaty was engraved on a metal disc. The words of the treaty were written in five different-size circles. Each circle fit inside the other. Today five linked rings are the symbol of the Olympics.

During the early games, records of the winners were not kept. The first champion of an Olympic game was recorded in 776 B.C. An athlete named Coroebus (kuh-REE-bus) won the one-*stade* (stayed) race. A stade is a little more than 200 yards. Thousands of people cheered Coroebus as he was crowned with a wreath of wild olive leaves.

The winner of the stade was also given the privilege of lighting the flame at a special altar in honor of Zeus. Each 4-year period between the games (called the *olympiad*) was named in honor of the winner of the stade.

In the first Olympics there was only a simple foot race, and just people from the area came. The celebration lasted one day. As time went on, new events were added to the games. More and more people came to compete and watch, and the festival lasted five days. One of the new events was the 2-stade race. Still later, a longer race was introduced, covering 15,210 feet or about three miles.

Then more events were added—boxing, wrestling, chariot racing, discus throwing, javelin throwing, jumping, and races for runners wearing armor. (A discus is circular and is thicker in the center than at the rim. A javelin is like a spear.) There were even contests for trumpeters.

A stade was said to have been the distance that Herakles could walk in one breath.

Coin showing the head of Zeus

The ancient games became a very exciting event. They were a religious ceremony, an athletic meet, and a carnival all rolled into one. Every 4 years, just before the start of the games, the area around the Olympia valley would become crowded with contestants and spectators from many other countries. They lived in tents or slept out under the stars. Magicians performed tricks, acrobats tumbled, and shopkeepers sold all kinds of food from colorful booths. The games became so popular that many famous people came to see them. The philosopher Socrates (SOCK-ruh-teez), the poet Pindar (PIN-der), the sculptor Phidias (FID-ee-us), and the historian Herodotus (heh-ROD-uh-tus) all attended the Olympic games.

In honor of the games, beautiful temples, altars, and statues were built in the Olympia valley. The most important temple was the Olympium. In it there was a huge statue of Zeus that was carved by Phidias. It was 40 feet tall and made of ivory and gold. The second most important temple was called the Heraeum (hih-REE-um). It was in honor of the goddess Hera (HEER-uh), the wife of Zeus. The wreaths of olive leaves that would be awarded to the champions were placed on tables in this temple.

The huge arenas in which the Olympics were held were in the Olympia valley. On one side of the temples were the stadium and hippodrome. The foot races were in the stadium. The hippodrome was the place where the horse races were held. On the other side of the temples were the *palaestra* (puh-LESS-truh) and the gymnasium. Wrestlers trained at the palaestra. The other athletes did their final training in the gymnasium.

There were slaves in Greece in ancient times, and they were not allowed to enter the games. Only free-born Greek males could compete in the contests. In fact, slaves and women were not even allowed to watch. Punishment for breaking this rule would be swift and terrible. If a woman was discovered at the Olympic games she would be pushed off a high cliff.

Only once was the no-women rule

disobeyed. A woman named Pherenice (feh-ruh-NIECE) of Rhodes went to the games to watch her son, Pisidores (PIS-ih-door-es), compete. She was disguised as a male athlete. Her son won and she was so excited that she rushed to congratulate him. Her robe slipped and she was discovered! Pherenice was only spared from death when the officials learned that her father and brothers had all been Olympic champions.

Getting ready for those ancient Olympics was just as difficult then as it is today. The athletes had to practice in their home cities for at least 10 months. They stayed on strict diets. They ate lots of cheese and drank only water. Trainers kept a watchful eye on them to make sure that they practiced faithfully. The best athletes in each sport were taken to Olympia for another month of hard training before the games began.

Winners of Olympic events were treated like heroes when they returned to their home cities. They received gifts, and parades and great feasts were held in their honor. If an athlete won three Olympic events, a life-size statue of him was set up in his city. A city would often be so proud of an Olympic winner that its citizens would break a hole through the city wall to let the hero enter. This showed that the athlete was so powerful that the city would be safe even with a hole in its protective wall.

The greatest honors were saved for the pentathlon (pen-TATH-lon) champions. The pentathlon was a series of five events—jumping, javelin throwing, discus throwing, foot racing, and wrestling. The discus, long jump, javelin, and foot race were the first four events. If anyone won three of these events, the contest was over and he was declared the winner of the pentathlon. If no one won three events, one more event was held—wrestling. Athletes who had finished well in the first four events competed in this contest.

Wrestling was an easy sport to judge. The man who threw his opponent to the ground three times was the winner. If both wrestlers hit the ground at the same time, the fall did not count. Wrestling on the ground was not allowed at all.

In most events there were not many injuries. However, the chariot races could be dangerous. In one race, only one of the nine starting charioteers managed to finish the race. Of course, he was the winner!

There were two other contests in which serious injury—or even death—was always possible. One was boxing and the other was a fierce sport called *pancratium* (pan-KRAY-shih-um), a combination of boxing and wrestling.

When fighters boxed, they wrapped strips of leather around their fists. The leather was often covered with pieces of metal. Unlike today, the boxers were not matched by weight. So usually the bigger and heavier man would win. A boxing bout continued until one of the boxers surrendered.

Everything was permitted in the pancratium. An athlete had to be very

Chariot racing was the only event in which a woman could be declared the winner. The rule was that whoever owned the team of horses was the victor. So a woman could be an Olympic champion, even though she could not attend the games.

Seats for judges at Olympia stadium

strong just to survive a pancratium contest, much less win. During one match, a boxing champion named Arrachion (ah-RACK-ee-on) grabbed his opponent's foot and began to twist it furiously. His opponent grabbed Arrachion by the throat. It was a life-and-death struggle. Arrachion was being strangled, but with one final effort he twisted the other wrestler's leg so severely that his opponent raised one arm to signal defeat. Just as he did so, Arrachion choked. Even though he was dead, Arrachion was still declared the winner!

There were many powerfully strong men who entered the pancratium and many legends about their great strength. Poulydamas (pa-LIH-di-mas) of the city of Thessaly once killed a lion with his bare hands on Mount Olympus. Another time, it is said that he stopped a speeding horse-drawn chariot in its tracks.

Theagenes (thea-AH-gen-eez) of the city of Thasos was another pancratium champion. He also won events in boxing and foot racing. Theagenes was so strong as a child that when he was just 9 years old, he carried home a huge bronze statue to prove his strength. Then he carried it back again, walking miles and miles each way. During his career, he was said to have won a grand total of 1,400 championships.

The Greeks honored all Olympic champions with stories and poems about their strength and skill. Every city and province wanted an Olympic winner because the Greeks believed that winners were favored by the gods. They also felt that their city would be treated with special kindness by the gods. The Olympic games grew in popularity. Contestants started to come from Rome, Africa, and Asia. Sadly, the tradition of honor and individual athletic skill began to disappear from the games. Instead, cities hired professional athletes to represent them. Judges could be bribed to declare certain athletes the winners.

Then the Romans began to conquer the cities of Greece. They enjoyed spectacular events and they loved the Olympics. The emperor of Rome, Nero, even took part in one of the Olympic chariot races. Even though he fell out of his chariot the Greeks allowed him to win. They did this because they feared he would put them to death if he lost. Although records were kept of the Olympic games that year, they were later removed from the record books.

Still later, Greece was invaded by barbarians from the north. The fine athletes of Greece were needed as soldiers and could not compete in the games. Finally, in A.D. 394 the games were outlawed by the Christian emperor of Rome, Theodosius I (THEA-uh-DOUGH-shus). Then more barbarians came to the valley and robbed the temples of their treasures.

The ancient Olympic games ended when the high ideals of the games were no longer respected. However, the standards and strivings for all Olympic athletes had been set. The motto of the Olympics today is **Swifter, Higher, Stronger.**

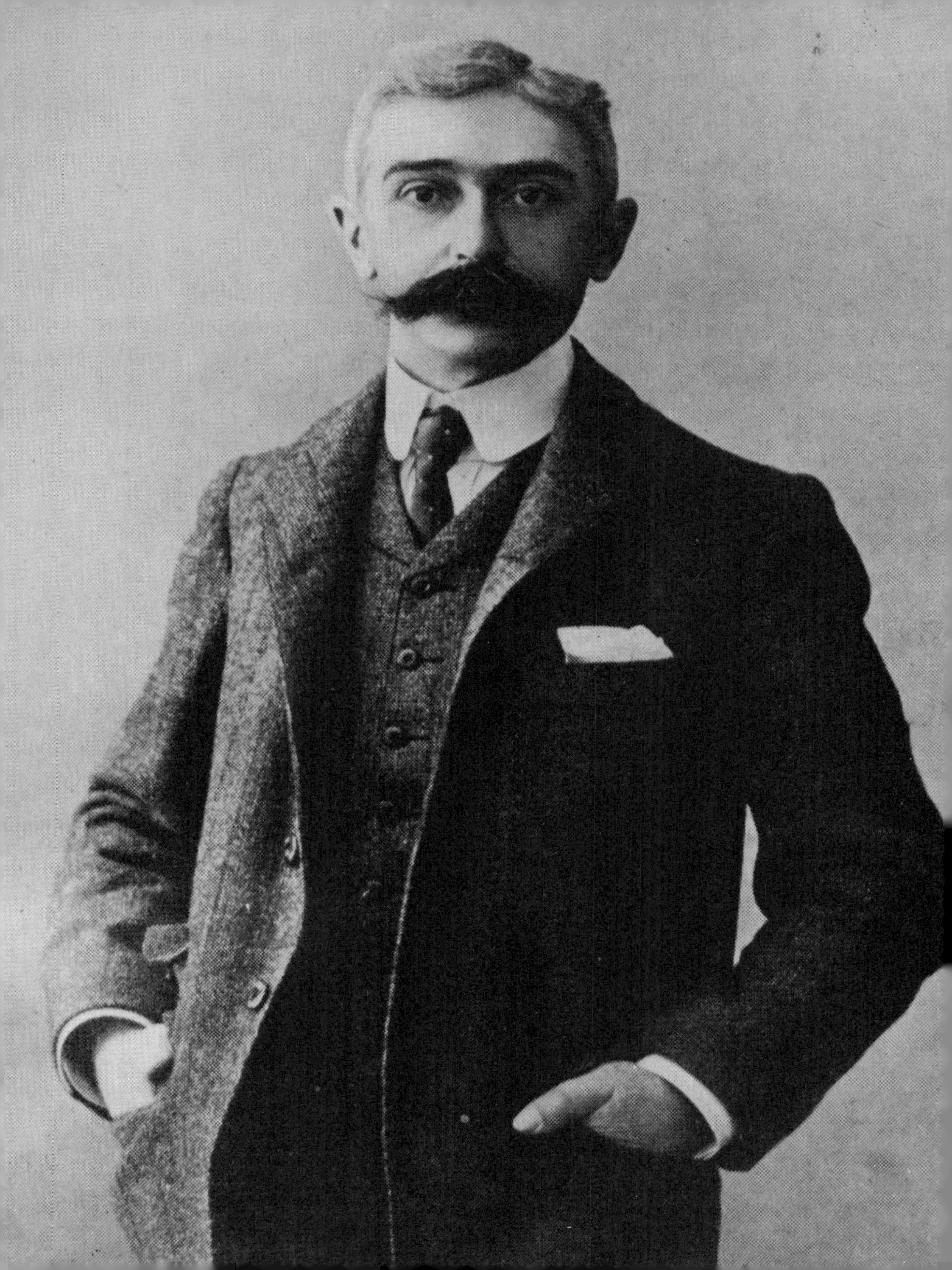

2

The Modern Olympics

The ancient Olympic games had ended in A.D. 394, but their influence did not end then. Legends and stories of Olympic heroes kept alive the inspiring Olympic ideals. Pindar's poems of praise to Olympic winners were studied and admired. People also admired the athletic beauty in Greek and Roman art. So, even though the games were not held, their greatness was remembered.

The beautiful temples and buildings in the Olympia valley were gone. Earthquakes and floods had damaged and covered them up. No one knew exactly where the site of the games had been.

But in 1829 a group of French archaeologists (are-key-OL-uh-gists) dug up parts of the great Temple of Zeus. This discovery made everyone interested in the Olympics again. In 1859, a wealthy Greek named Evgenios Zappas started games modeled after the Olympics. His attempt was a failure. The games were badly organized. The events were held in the streets of Athens, and spectators were injured in the pushing and shoving. In 1870 more games were tried, but they were also unsuccessful.

Between 1875 and 1881 a team of German archaeologists uncovered the entire area that had once been the site of the great temples and stadium. One of the visitors to the excavation was a young Frenchman named Baron Pierre de Coubertin (pea-AIR de coo-behr-TAN). He was a scholar and educator,

Baron Pierre de Coubertin

and admired the ancient Greek athletes.

Coubertin felt that physical fitness was an important part of education. And he dreamed of the day when people from all over the world would come together in the spirit of competition.

Baron de Coubertin tried to get people in France interested in the idea of physical education. When he was 26, he helped set up an organization that promoted the physical fitness of French school children. He traveled throughout Europe and the United States to see how other nations conducted school athletic programs.

In 1894, at a meeting of people from several countries, Coubertin suggested that the Olympics be started again. The delegates decided that the first modern Olympics would be held in 1896 in Athens—the capital of the country that had given the world the ancient Olympics. Every four years a different country would have the honor of hosting the games.

There were many problems for the new Olympic committee. There was no stadium in Greece, and the country could not afford to build one. Crown Prince Constantine of Greece asked for help from George Averoff, a wealthy Greek who often donated money for educational purposes. Averoff gave $386,000 so that the ancient Pan-Athenian stadium could be rebuilt. Greece raised more money for other expenses. About $65,000 came from public donations. Another $100,000 was raised by selling eight kinds of Olympic postage stamps.

The United States was having troubles of another kind. There was no official Olympic committee in America, so there was no official Olympic team. The New York Athletic Club, which included some of America's finest track athletes, did not want to take part in the Olympics. It seemed that the United States would be unable to send anyone to Greece for the first modern Olympic games. But a Princeton University history professor named William Milligan Sloane, a friend of Coubertin, saved the day.

Sloane explained the problem to Robert Garrett, a shot-putter and captain of Princeton's track-and-field team, and talked him into entering the Olympics. Garrett, in turn, convinced pole vaulter Albert Tyler, sprinter Francis Lane, and quarter-miler Herbert Jamison to join the team. (The shot-put is an event in which an athlete throws a heavy metal ball. In pole vaulting the athlete uses a pole to swing himself over a bar. A sprinter runs as fast as he can because he has to cover only a short distance.)

Five members of the Boston Athletic Club decided that competing in the Olympics was a good idea—jumper Ellery Clark, pole vaulter William Hoyt, sprinter Tom Burke, hurdler Tom Curtis, and distance runner Arthur Blake.

Another volunteer was James Connolly, a jumper at Harvard. Since the Olympics would be held in April, right in the middle of the spring school term, Connolly asked for time off from school. Harvard refused permission and Connolly became so angry he quit the school, never to return there as a student.

Completing the team was a swimmer named Gardner Williams, and two brothers, army captains John and Summer Paine, who entered the shooting competition.

Some events of the Olympics were new to the Americans. Robert Garrett decided the discus event was for him. But he had never even seen a real discus. From pictures he found in his school library, and with a friend's help, he designed and made a discus. Garrett practiced for several weeks, but he did not expect to do very well.

It took more than two weeks for the "unofficial" American team to reach Athens. They traveled by ship to France, and then by train to Athens. Arriving just in time for the Olympic games, they had no time to practice.

The opening ceremony of the first modern Olympics was very exciting. A crowd of 50,000 people watched as a

William Hoyt

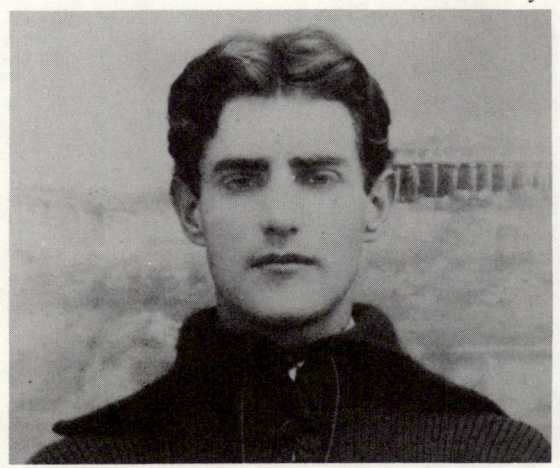

Robert Garrett

torch, which had been carried by relay runners from the Olympia valley, was brought into the stadium. The torch-bearer climbed a series of steps and lighted the eternal flame. A choir sang the Olympic hymn. Athletes from 13 nations marched into the stadium and were greeted by wildly cheering crowds and the King of Greece. After 1,502 years, the Olympic games were being held again.

The United States team, poorly trained and tired from the long trip, was not expected to win many events. To the surprise of everyone, the Americans almost ran away with the Olympic games.

First James Connolly won the triple jump. The triple jump is really a hop, step, and jump. The athlete runs up to a mark—hops, steps, and then jumps as far as he or she can. Next, surprisingly enough, Robert Garrett won the discus event. The discus he had made and trained with was actually about a pound heavier than the official discus. So it was easy for him to throw the lighter one. Garrett also won the shot-put later in the games.

The American team won almost all the track-and-field events. Sprinter Tom Burke won the 100-meter (about 300 feet) and 400-meter (about 1,200 feet) races; hurdler Tom Curtis took the 110-meter hurdles; Bill Hoyt won the pole vault. The Americans placed first, second, and third in the running broad jump and running high jump. Ellery Clark won both events. Between them, Garrett and Connolly won second and third in both contests. The Americans took no prizes in the 800-meter race, but Arthur Blake placed second in the 1,500-meter race.

All the Americans were outstanding. The army captains took three first places in shooting, while swimmer

A French sprinter wore gloves in his 100-meter race because he was running before the royalty of Greece.

Anxious to finish first in the marathon, the Greeks offered many prizes to any Greek who won. The wealthy George Averoff promised a huge sum of money and his daughter in marriage. Other prizes were a barrel of rare wine, free trips to the barber for life, and 2,000 pounds of chocolate!

Gardner Williams was second in the 100-meter free-style event.

Many of the Greek spectators felt disappointed. The Greeks had invented track-and-field events, but the United States team was doing better than the Greeks. There was just one last chance for a Greek victory—the marathon, a 26-mile race. Their champion was a 25-year-old named Spiridon Loues, who was a country shepherd.

At the start of the marathon, Loues fell far behind. But, cheered on by spectators lining the roads, he began to catch up. The lead runners began to slow down or drop out, and Loues continued to run smoothly. As he trotted into the stadium, ahead of the rest of the runners, the crowd went wild with joy. The two princes of Greece, George and Constantine, came out of the stands and ran the last few yards alongside Loues. The ancient honor of Greece was saved. In fact, 5 of the first 6 finishers in the marathon that day were Greeks.

On the last day of the Olympics, each champion was presented with a gold medal and an olive branch. The winners, led by Spiridon Loues, marched proudly around the stadium, while the crowds cheered. The games were a great triumph for Pierre de Coubertin, for the Greek nation, and for all the athletes. Today, gold, silver, and bronze medals are awarded for first, second, and third places in each event.

Spiridon Loues, Greek winner of first Olympic marathon race

25

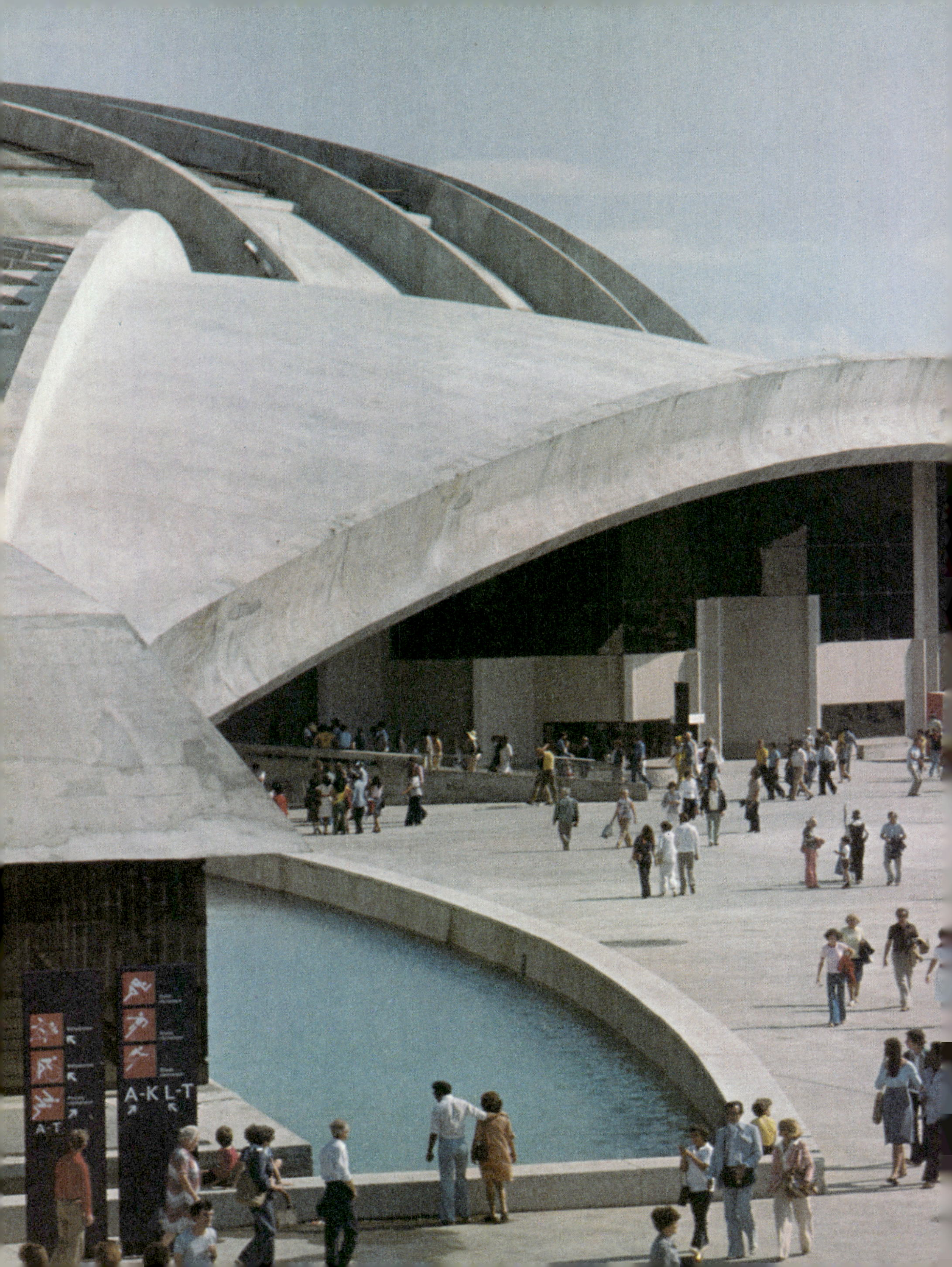
A-KL-T
A-T

Olympic Preparations

Planning for the 1896 Olympics was easy compared to what has to be done for the games today.

In 1896, a few nations and their athletes took part. Few spectators came from foreign countries, and there were plenty of hotel rooms for everyone. No women were entered in any of the events. Winter sports were still in the future. There weren't many reporters, and newspapers around the world did not print many stories about what was happening in Athens.

But today, preparing for the Olympics is a tremendously complicated job for the host nation and the athletes. Many millions of dollars are spent organizing the winter and summer games.

Thousands of athletes must be fed and housed during the Olympics. An Olympic village has to be built for them. Tons of food must be shipped to the host city. But not everyone can eat the same kind of food! The Israeli and Arab athletes' religions forbid them to eat pork products of any kind. Members of certain religious sects in India may not eat beef. And people from different countries enjoy eating different kinds of bread, spices, and vegetables. Sometimes even a change in drinking water can upset an athlete's physical condition, so some nations supply their athletes with bottled water.

The thousands of visitors who attend the Olympics have to be taken care of,

Swimming hall at the 1976 Montreal summer Olympics

too. That means building more hotels and restaurants. Sometimes these tourists come in their own cars, causing terrible traffic jams. Selling tickets is a problem, especially for the more popular events. People often order their tickets more than a year in advance.

More difficulties are caused by the arrival of newspaper and magazine reporters and photographers. Then there are the people from various television networks around the world. Huge trailers full of electronic equipment must be parked close to the arenas and ski slopes. Miles and miles of telephone cables are needed and thousands of telephones must be installed. An additional supply of electricity is needed for the new hotels, restaurants, and athletes' buildings.

The winter Olympics and the summer Olympics each present different problems.

One of the greatest problems faced by a host city for the winter Olympics is the weather. Because it is so cold, construction of buildings is not possible for about 6 months of the year. Therefore, all the buildings must be built during the warmer months. Sometimes, even the coldest areas do not get enough snow when it is needed. Special snow-making equipment must be on hand to spray the ski slopes.

All the construction and equipment are very expensive. It will probably cost about $150,000,000 to prepare for the 1980 winter Olympics at Lake Placid, New York.

Summer Olympics present their own set of difficulties. The crowds are usually larger. Many people plan their vacations so that they can attend some of the events. Huge amounts of money are spent to build a new stadium, field houses, and swimming pools.

The host cities have 4 years to prepare for games that will last for only 2 weeks. But the athletes take much longer to get ready for the Olympics. They usually begin training before they become teenagers.

Nadia Comaneci of Romania was only 14 years old when she made her perfect scores in the 1976 Olympics. But she had been practicing gymnastics since she was 6 years old. America's Debbie Meyer trained hard for years before she won her three gold medals in swimming at the age of 16 during the

The construction for the 1976 summer games in Montreal, Canada, cost more than $100,000,000.

1968 Olympics. The many thousands of athletes who hope to be chosen for their country's Olympic team must work and train hard for a long time.

Almost all nations choose an Olympic squad in the same way. The athletes go through a series of tryouts. At special track meets, boxing matches, or team-sport practice games, the best contestants are chosen by the various coaches who will help train them for the Olympics. If they are sprinters, their time trials are carefully checked. Swimmers are studied for form and speed. Gymnasts are graded just as they would be in the real Olympics.

Nations such as Russia have some advantages in team sports. Their basketball team, for example, is formed long before the actual games. They can practice together for a long time. Each player gets to know what his teammates can do.

Things are different in the United States. The American team is made up of the best college players. Before entering the Olympics, they must complete their studies or get a leave of absence. They have much less time to practice together as a team.

The 1960 Olympic basketball team is a good example of a super team that was made up of players from many different colleges. At the guard positions were two players who would wind up in basketball's Hall of Fame—Oscar Robertson and Jerry West. Other members of the team included Walt Bellamy, Bob Boozer, Terry Dischinger, Darrall Imhoff, Jerry Lucas, John Havlicek, and Jay Arnette. All but two of the players came from different schools.

Some nations always seem to be among the leaders in certain sports. The Russians usually have outstanding hockey teams and championship weight lifters. From 1928 through 1960, Hungarians won the saber (fencing) event. Japanese men have won gymnastics medals many times. The United States does particularly well in the decathlon and various track events.

But all the problem solving, all the training, all the planning, and all the building prove worthwhile when the parade begins that opens the Olympic games.

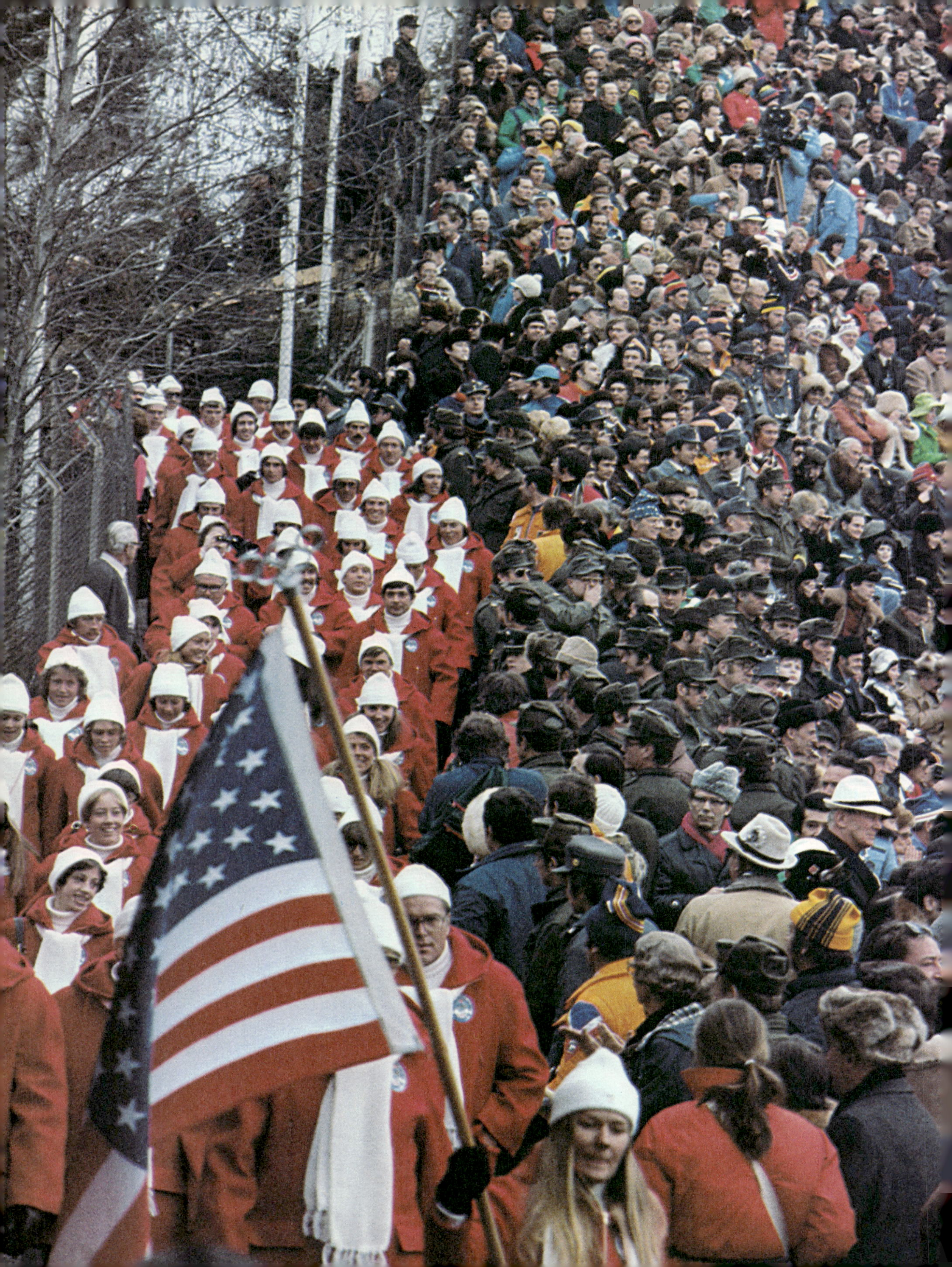

4

The Opening Olympic Ceremony

The opening ceremony of the Olympic games is one of the most colorful festivals in the world of sports.

In the Olympia valley in Greece, weeks before the games start, a woman dressed in ancient Greek robes lights a torch—an Olympic flame—by using the rays of the sun. The torch is handed to a runner, who is the first member of the relay team. He runs with the torch and passes it to the next runner. Runner after runner brings the torch closer to the host city. As the final runner approaches the stadium, crowded with anxiously waiting fans, the president of the International Olympic Committee turns to the head of state of the host country and says, "I have the honor to invite you to proclaim open the Games of the Olympiad of the modern era, initiated by the Baron Pierre de Coubertin in 1896."

The head of state then declares that the Olympic games may begin.

> The five-ringed Olympic flag was adopted in 1913. The rings symbolize the unity of the five continents. At least one of the colors—blue, black, red, yellow, and green—of the rings appears in the flag of each member country.

Parade of athletes at 1976 Innsbruck winter Olympics

The bands strike up, and the great parade of athletes begins. The Olympic flag bearer leads the procession. The first group in the line of march is the team from Greece. As the founders of the Olympics, they have the honor of leading the parade. The teams from the rest of the nations that are taking part march into the stadium by country in alphabetical order. One member of each team carries the national flag. Often a team will wear the traditional clothing of their country. The last team in the parade is from the host country. The entire parade, hundreds and hundreds of athletes, marches around the stadium to the cheers and applause of the crowd.

Flocks of doves, the symbol of peace and good fellowship, are freed during the parade. They fill the stadium with the whirring sound of their wings.

At the end of the ceremonies, the torch from Olympia is carried into the stadium. The torch has been kept lit even if it has had to cross oceans. In 1956 the lighted torch was flown from Greece to Australia. For the 1976 Montreal Olympics, something new was tried. A duplicate of the torch in Greece was brought to Ottawa, Canada, and it was lit by a strong beam of light—a laser

The Olympic oath is repeated by one representative from each team during the opening ceremonies. He or she says: "We swear that we will take part in these Olympic games in the true spirit of sportsmanship, and that we will respect and abide by the rules that govern them, for the glory of sport and the honor of our country."

beam—all the way from Europe.

This newly lit torch was brought into the stadium in Montreal. It was held high by a young man and a young woman from Canada, running side by side. As they entered the stadium, the cheers of the vast crowd thundered. Very slowly they ran around the oval track, and then up the steps to the top of a huge platform where a giant vaselike container was waiting. The container held fuel that would burn for a long time. The lighted torch was touched to the fuel and the Olympic flame was lit.

Another Olympic competition had begun.

Arrival of Olympic torch at opening ceremony for the 1976 Montreal summer Olympics

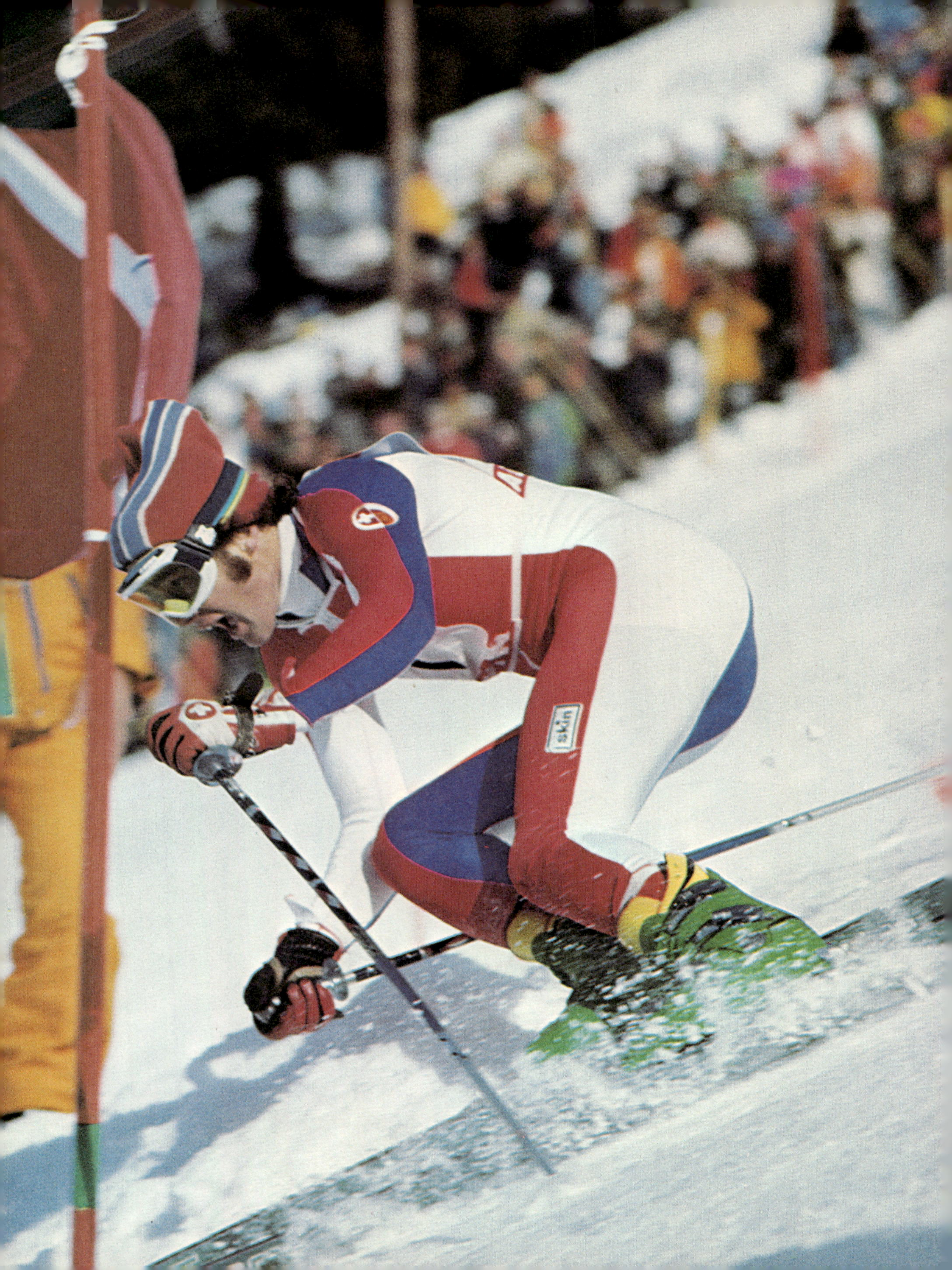
skin

The Winter Olympics

For a long time, winter sports were not a part of the Olympic games. In 1908 figure skating was included in the London Olympics, but very few people were interested.

In 1920 winter sports were more popular, and the International Olympic Committee decided to add figure skating, ice hockey, and skiing to the games at Antwerp.

The winter sports were so successful that the committee planned a separate Olympics for winter games only. And, in 1924, at Chamonix, France, the first winter games were tried! The experiment was a great success. The winter Olympics had begun.

The first winter Olympic games included ice hockey, figure skating, speed skating, cross-country skiing, ski jumping, and bobsledding. Since then, tobogganing, downhill and slalom (SLAH-lum) skiing, and the biathlon (bye-ATH-lon) have been added to the thrilling winter games.

To compete in the biathlon, an athlete must be an expert skier and marksman. There are four targets on a 20-kilometer cross-country ski course (about 12 miles.) The skier stops and shoots five times at each target, which is from 100 to 250 meters (about 300 to 750 feet) away. Each time he misses, two minutes are added to his total time. The skier who finishes the course with the best time is the winner.

Skier streaks through slalom gates

Sonja Henie

One of the first great ice skaters in the winter Olympics was Sonja Henie, an 11-year-old who was the Norwegian figure-skating champion. In the 1924 games Sonja finished last, but that never happened again.

There are two parts to an Olympic figure-skating competition. All skaters must skate the special "school figures." The skaters perform certain set skating movements that test their skill, and judges give points to each competitor. This part counts 60 percent of the final score. The scoring by points depends on each judge's opinion. There is no time clock to choose the fastest person. There is no tape to measure the athlete who goes farthest. The winner is the one who the judges think skates the best. The skater with the highest overall score is the winner.

The second part, which counts for 40 percent of the final score, is "free skating." Sonja felt that free skating needed more style and grace. She studied ballet, and added the beautiful spins and leaps of the ballet to her routine.

The audience and the judges loved Sonja's performance in the 1928 Olympics and she won easily. From then on, other figure skaters added dance movements to their figure skating.

Sonja, called "The Norwegian Doll," won the championship in 1932 at Lake Placid, New York, and then she won again for the third time in a row in 1936 at Garmisch-Partenkirchen.

Sonja Henie became a professional athlete after her figure-skating victory in the 1936 Olympics. She was the richest former Olympic champion in history—she earned $47,500,000.

Alexei Ulanov and Irina Rodnina, Russian winners of the 1972 gold medal for pairs figure skating

Peggy Fleming, U.S. winner of the 1968 gold medal for women's figure skating

Rosi Mittermaier, West German winner of the 1976 gold medal for women's slalom race

Alpine skiing events were first introduced to the Olympics in 1948. There were three kinds of races: giant slalom, special slalom, and downhill.

In the downhill and slalom events, the skiers do not compete against each other. They race against the clock. Only one skier at a time goes over the course. The skier with the fastest time is the winner.

In slalom races, the skier must pass through a series of flags known as "gates." The gates are set up in a zigzag pattern and they test the ability of the skier to turn quickly and well.

One of the greatest Alpine skiers was Austria's Anton Sailer. He proved his wonderful skiing ability in the 1956 Olympics at Cortina d'Ampezzo, Italy.

Toni was born in Kitzbühel, in the Austrian Alps. He began to ski when he was only 2 years old. He was 20 years old when he entered the 1956 Olympics.

Weather conditions were not good at Cortina d'Ampezzo that year. There had been no snow in the area for more than three weeks and the Italian government started to haul in snow from other regions. All of a sudden the snow began to come down—over a foot of snow fell. The games could begin.

The slopes were icy-slick and dangerous, but Toni Sailer had practiced under icy conditions many times.

The first event was the giant slalom. The course was nearly 1,000 meters (about two-thirds of a mile) long and the start of the run was about 2,000 feet higher than the finish. He and the other skiers had to zigzag through seventy-one gates.

Toni's teammate, Anderl Molterer, was also from Kitzbühel. Molterer whizzed down the course in record time. But Toni Sailer was 6 seconds faster and won the event.

The special slalom was next. There were two runs—the first with seventy-nine gates, the second with ninety-two. Toni Sailer scored the fastest time and he won his second gold medal.

Finally, there was the long downhill. This course was more than 3,200 meters (about 2 miles), and the start was 3,000

Rosi Mittermaier from West Germany wins a second gold medal for the 1976 women's downhill race.

feet higher than the finish. It was full of ice and the surface was uneven. The course was so difficult that fifty-eight of the seventy-five skiers fell down at least once. Sailer almost fell a few times, but somehow he managed not only to keep his balance, but to win his third straight gold medal.

In 1968, twelve years after Toni Sailer had won all three Alpine skiing events, a young Frenchman named Jean-Claude Killy did the same thing.

Ski jumping is one of the Nordic events. The skier does not use ski poles. Jumping skis are longer, heavier, and wider than ordinary skis. The bindings are looser, so that the skier's heels can rise up when the jumper leans forward.

The jumper pushes off and skis down the ramp gathering speed, until he reaches the lip or takeoff point. The jumper soars into the air with his arms close to his sides and his body leaning slightly forward. He then lands on the sloped landing hill and skis to the finish.

Ski jumping

Facing page: Jean-Claude Killy, 1968 French winner of gold medals for men's downhill, slalom, and giant slalom races

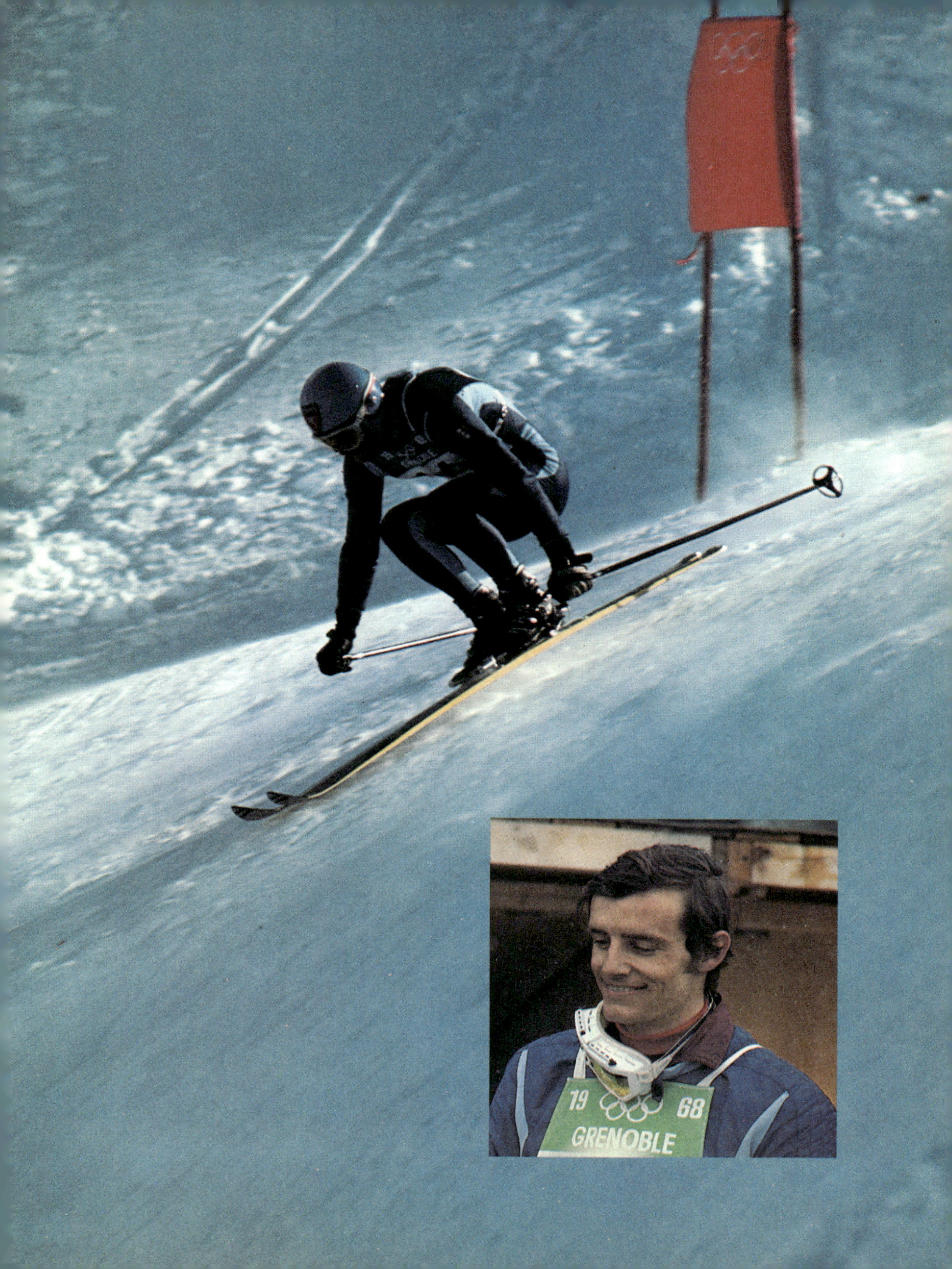
19 68
GRENOBLE

Cross-country skiing

Cross-country skiing is also a Nordic event. It is a race over rolling terrain. Men's races cover from 15 to 50 kilometers (9.3 to 31 miles), women's races cover from 5 to 10 kilometers (3.1 to 6.2 miles).

One of the most dangerous of all winter events is the bobsledding race. The sleds hurtle down the course and around the turns at over 90 miles per hour. There is always the chance that the bobsled will go over the top of the icy wall and crash.

One of the sledders in the 1932 Olympics at Lake Placid was an American named Eddie Eagan. Eagan had won a gold medal in the 1920 Olympics as a light-heavyweight boxer. He then entered a sport in which he had never competed.

Eagan and his bobsledding teammates won the gold medal. It was the first and only time anyone won gold medals in the winter and summer Olympics.

Tobogganing is another winter sport very similar to bobsledding. The *luge* (loozh) is a very lightweight sled. The athlete lies on his back, feet first, and goes down the course. Steering is done with the feet and by shifting body weight.

Eugenio Monti of Italy won two gold,
two silver, and two bronze Olympic medals
in bobsled competitions from 1956 to 1968.

Bobsledding

Bobsled going into sharp turn

44

Tobogganing

Sometimes one country keeps winning a particular event for a while. Ice hockey is a good example. Canada was the champion in 1920 when hockey was added to the Olympic games. The Canadians won the gold medal four straight times. But in 1936, Britain was the surprise winner. There were no Olympics for the next twelve years because of the two world wars. But in 1948, and again in 1952, the Canadians were the winners.

In 1956 the Russians began to play great hockey. They won the gold medal. It seemed that they were going to be strong enough to win all the time.

Hockey

The United States' hockey team in 1960 was a strange mix. There were some college players, two insurance salesmen, an advertising man, a fireman, a carpenter, and a soldier. Many of them had never played in international competition.

But the Americans managed to beat a strong Czechoslovakian team, coming from behind to pull out a victory. Then the United States clobbered the Australian squad and went on to beat Sweden and Germany. They even upset the powerful Russian team.

Only one game remained to be played for the championship. It was a re-match against Czechoslovakia. The Czechs had recovered after their loss to the Americans and had beaten all their other opponents.

The Americans were tired. The Olympic site at Squaw Valley was a mile above sea level, so it was difficult to breathe. The United States' squad went into their dressing room at the end of the second period, trailing 4–3.

During the time-out, a Russian player named Nikolai Sologubov walked in.

Canada's hockey team has won the Olympic title six times: in 1920, 1924, 1928, 1932, 1948, and 1952.

Sologubov spoke little English, but he had become quite friendly with the Americans. He managed to make them understand that they would have an advantage if they breathed pure oxygen.

The Americans followed his suggestion. It worked! They went back out on the ice and swarmed all over the Czech defense. In the third period the Americans banged home six goals, while the Czechs didn't score at all. The Americans won 9–4, and took the gold medal in ice hockey.

The outstanding Russian team came back to win the next three ice-hockey gold medals in 1964, 1968, and 1972.

Sometimes it is difficult to understand the winter games because there are so many fine points. In ski jumping, for example, judges decide whether the jumper's body is in the correct position while the skier is in the air. Points are awarded for good form. The distance jumped also counts in picking the medalists.

But everyone understands speed skating. It's a race on ice skates, the same as a sprint or long-distance run on a track.

Sheila Young, U.S. winner of the 1976 gold medal for women's 500-meter speed-skating race

Speed skaters have been clocked at speeds of over 30 miles per hour.

Speed skating

Lidija Skoblikova, Russian speed skater

One of the greatest of all speed skaters in the history of the Olympics was a young Russian girl from the Ural Mountains. Her name is Lidija Skoblikova. Lidija won gold medals in the 1,500-meter (about 4,000 feet) and the 3,000-meter races in the 1960 Olympics. She finished fourth in the 1,000-meter race. It was in 1964 at Innsbruck that she astonished the sports world. There were only four speed-skating events for women and she won them all: the 500-meter, the 1,000-meter, the 1,500-meter, and the 3,000-meter events. It was the first time that anyone had won four gold medals in the winter Olympics.

John Curry, British winner of the 1976 gold medal for men's figure skating

Dorothy Hamill, U.S. winner of the 1976 gold medal for women's figure skating

Tenley Albright, U.S. winner of the 1956 gold medal for women's figure skating

Olympic athletes are people who are used to hard work and long hours of practice in their striving for excellence. Tenley Albright, an American figure skater, was one such woman of determination. In the 1952 Olympics at Oslo, sixteen-year-old Tenley won runner-up honors. Then she attended Radcliffe College as a pre-medical student. Tenley planned to become a doctor like her father, who was a surgeon in Boston. She also planned to return to the Olympics for a shot at the gold medal.

In 1956, while training for the event which was still two weeks away, Tenley slipped. Her left skate cut deeply into her right ankle. Tenley's father was called to Cortina, Italy, to treat her. Although the wound was not completely healed and still painful, Tenley competed in the Olympics. Tenley ignored the ache in her ankle. She went out on the ice and skated to a close victory over Carol Heiss. Carol, in turn, went on to win the gold medal in 1960.

Millions of fans around the world follow the excitement on the slopes, rinks, and runs of the winter games. At the end of the winter Olympics, the athletes return home—some with medals and some with the ambition to come back in four years. But the winter Olympic games are just the start of a spectacular year of Olympic sports competition. There is much more to come—the even bigger summer games!

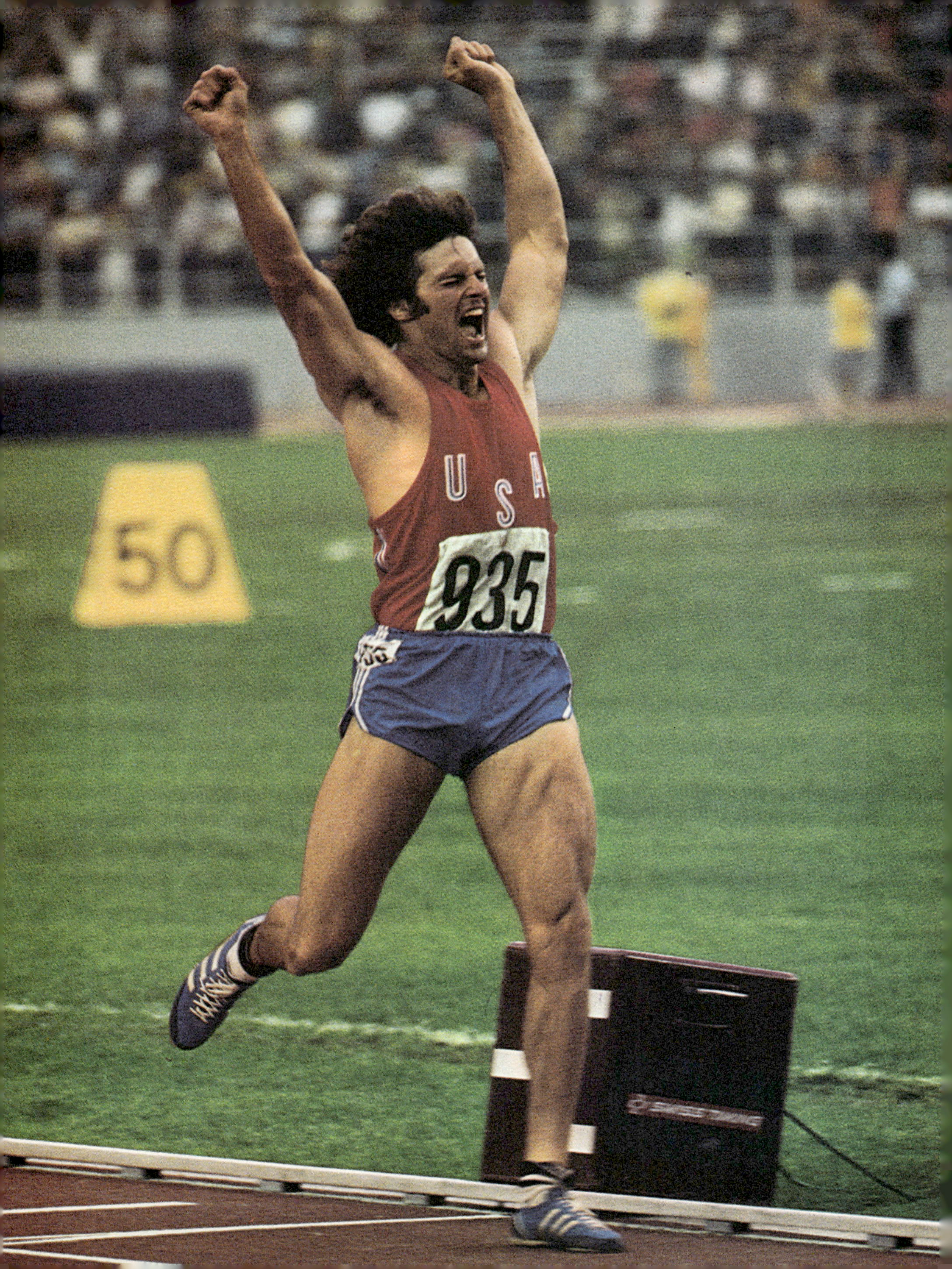
USA
935
50

The Summer Olympics

The summer Olympic games are a little like a five-ring circus because there are many, many events packed into a short period of time. Athletes compete on the track, various playing fields, and courts, in gymnasiums, and in and on the water.

Of all the events, gymnastics have become one of the favorites to watch. The amazing skill and beauty of the young gymnasts have captured the attention of the world.

One of the most popular and exciting gymnasts to compete in recent years is Nadia Comaneci from Romania. Fourteen-year-old Nadia burst on the Olympic scene when she competed in 1976 in Montreal against Olga Korbut, the great young Russian gymnast. Olga had won two gold medals in the 1972 Olympics. In 1976 Olga was going to try to repeat her victories.

As Nadia watched, Olga approached the uneven parallel bars. They are called uneven bars because they are at different heights. The upper bar is 7½ feet from the floor; the lower bar is about 5 feet from the floor.

Olga Korbut leaped up, caught hold of one bar, and began her routine. She flipped, twisted, and turned. The crowd cheered when she finished her routine. The judges awarded Olga a score of 9:90. It would take almost a perfect score of 10:00 to beat Olga.

Nadia was next. She jumped and

Bruce Jenner, winner of the 1976 decathlon, raises his arms in victory.

grabbed the lower bar. She performed an incredible series of whirls and spins. She made a dazzling dismount, and stood straight as an arrow.

The crowd applauded Nadia wildly. The judges were astonished by Nadia's performance and gave her a perfect score of 10:00! It was the first perfect gymnastic score in the history of the Olympic games.

The balance beam was scheduled for the next day. The balance beam is a piece of padded wood, about 16 feet long and only 4 inches wide. Women gymnasts perform remarkable acrobatic tricks on this very narrow beam.

Nadia Comaneci of Romania performs on the uneven parallel bars (*top*) and balance beam (*bottom*). Nadia ends her floor exercise routine (*right*).

54

Olga Korbut of Russia performs in the floor exercise event.

When it was Nadia's turn, she leaped up on the beam and stood very still for a moment on one foot. Then she performed a handstand. She stepped and skipped, flipped and cartwheeled, and executed a wide split before her dismount.

Once again Nadia Comaneci was awarded a perfect score of 10:00!

Olga Korbut, the Russian star, tried her best. But the best she could score was 9:90.

The gymnasts competed the next day in the floor exercises. They perform their routines to music and must do very difficult tumbling and acrobatic tricks as well as dance movements. Nadia did her routine to the beat of jazz. Her routine wasn't good enough for a score of 10:00, but it did earn her third place and a bronze medal.

Nadia Comaneci won gold medals for the balance beam, the uneven bars, and for her performance in the all-around competition. She also helped Romania win the silver medal for team competition.

Even with her perfect scores, Nadia could not be called the greatest of all women gymnasts. That honor belongs to Larissa Latynina of the Soviet Union.

In 1956 Larissa took four gold medals

55

Nadia Comaneci received seven perfect scores of 10:00 at the 1976 Olympics—four were on the uneven parallel bars and the other three were on the balance beam.

and one silver in her events. In 1960 she won three gold medals, two silver medals, and one bronze medal. In 1964 she won two gold medals, two silver medals, and two bronze medals. In three Olympics Larissa Latynina earned nine gold medals, five silver medals, and three bronze medals.

Men gymnasts have also thrilled spectators in the summer Olympics.

While only women compete on the uneven parallel bars and balance beam, men and women compete in the floor exercises. They also compete in the vault. They take off from a springboard and vault (jump) over a leather object called a vaulting horse. The women vault over the width of the horse while the men vault over the whole length of the horse. There are no handles to hold on to and the gymnast must land on both feet.

Only men compete on the pommel horse because great strength is needed in the arms and shoulders for this event. The horse is 1.10 meters (about 3 feet 7 inches) high. When the gymnast begins his routine, he grabs the two handles, or pommels, and swings himself up. Then he keeps swinging back and forth with splits and circular movements. A competitor must swing his legs; he can't lift them. He may place his hands on the horse as well as on the pommels.

The rings are another event that requires a great deal of strength, so only men compete. The gymnast leaps up and catches the two rings that are suspended from the ceiling. His whole routine is performed in the air.

Men compete on the parallel bars, which are made of flexible wood. They are spaced about 18 inches apart and are 5 feet 7 inches above the floor. The horizontal or high bar is a little over 8 feet from the ground. Some of the most exciting and daring gymnastic routines are performed on the horizontal bar.

Men gymnasts performing on the parallel bars (*top left*), rings (*top right*), and pommel horse.

Training for any Olympic event is important if an athlete is going to win. Emil Zatopek, a track star from Czechoslovakia, was one athlete who believed in training hard. He would get up every day at six o'clock in the morning. Some days he would run 10 miles, some days as much as 25 miles. He was an army officer and he wore his heavy army boots when he ran. That gave his legs tremendous strength when he wore only light track shoes.

Zatopek was not only a great runner, he was also a great jokester. He especially liked to fool around during races. At the end of a long race, Zatopek would groan and stagger, as if he were ready to drop. But he wasn't even tired. He was just kidding the spectators.

Once, in an Olympic trial heat, he took the lead for a time, but then he slowed up. (A heat is a contest to eliminate some of the athletes so that there will be a small number competing in the

Emil Zatopek gasps his way to another victory.

Emil was not the only champion named Zatopek in the 1952 Olympics. His wife, Dana, won the gold medal in the women's javelin competition.

final race.) Zatopek allowed a few runners to get ahead of him. For a while, he ran beside an American.

Zatopek turned to the American and said, "Hurry up, you'll miss the bus." Then he increased his speed, and won the heat easily.

In the 1948 Olympics, when he was 25 years old, Zatopek won the 10,000-meter (6.2 miles) race and finished second in the 5,000 meters. But he showed the world what a great champion he was in 1952 at Helsinki.

First he entered the 10,000-meter race. For almost half the race he ran easily, far back among the rest. Then he leaped into the lead. But Zatopek had to have his little joke. With each stride he seemed ready to fall down and die. He wheezed and gasped. There was a look of pain on his face. Yet, whenever another runner came too close, Zatopek would zoom away as if his opponent were standing still. Nobody could catch him. His time was 29 minutes 17 seconds—he had beaten his own Olympic record by 42 seconds.

But Zatopek did not seem happy. "I am disappointed," he said to reporters. "I wasn't fast at all. I will try to do better in the 5,000-meter race."

Zatopek lagged behind in the 5,000-meter race, too. With about 1,000 meters to go, he started to charge ahead. As the runners rounded the final turn, Zatopek swung into an outside lane. He blazed his way into the lead and won the race. Zatopek broke the Olympic record by 9 seconds.

Emil Zatopek was not finished yet. He announced that he would enter the marathon—a distance of 26 miles 385 yards. He had never even tried to run in that event before.

Zatopek did not try his gasp-and-groan joke this time. He had something else in mind. He took the lead, and at the 15-mile mark he was far ahead.

He slowed down and let Jim Peters of Great Britain catch up. Many people thought Peters would win the marathon. Since Zatopek could speak several languages, he was able to talk to Peters.

Zatopek said, "I haven't run a marathon before, but don't you think we ought to go a bit faster?"

Zatopek won the race easily. He broke the record by more than 6 minutes. When the reporters asked him what he thought of running in a marathon, Zatopek said, "Really, it's a very boring race."

59

Otis Davis in 1960 with his gold medal for the 400-meter dash

Zatopek was sure that he could win any race he entered. Most athletes think they have a good chance. But not Otis Davis. In fact, Davis didn't think he was much good at all.

Davis was a student at the University of Oregon on a basketball scholarship. He wanted to find out how well he could do in track-and-field sports. He failed as a high jumper and he failed in the quarter-mile. (A high jumper must jump over a crossbar that is held up by two supporting bars.)

"You can't make a runner out of me," he told his coach, Bill Bowerman.

But Bowerman refused to let Davis quit. Davis kept working, and he kept improving. He became good enough to make the Olympic team as one of the 400-meter (about 1,300 feet) runners.

In the 1960 Rome Olympics, Davis qualified for the 400-meter final with a time of 45.5 seconds. Davis could hardly believe he had run that fast. "I can't do any better than that," he said. But he was wrong.

In the finals, Davis took the lead at the 200-meter mark. At the same time a runner named Carl Kaufmann from Germany began to challenge him. It was neck-and-neck. Kaufmann threw himself across the tape at the finish line. It seemed that both runners had crossed the line at the same time. Both runners were timed at 44.9 seconds.

After studying photographs of the finish, the judges awarded the race to Davis.

"I owe it all to Bill Bowerman," Davis said happily. "I never dreamed I could go this far." Both Davis and Kaufmann had broken the Olympic record for the 400-meter dash. It was broken 8 years

The winner of the 100-meter dash is often called "the fastest man on earth."

later by Lee Evans of the United States.

Americans usually do well in the sprints. American sprinters won the 100-meter (about 300 feet) dash and the 200-meter dash in all the games from 1932 through 1956. Americans lost both events in 1960, but won them again in 1964 and 1968. Sometimes an American has won both events during an Olympic meet. In 1932 Eddie Tolan took the gold medals in the 100 meters and the 200 meters. In 1936 it was a speed demon named Jesse Owens. In 1956 Bobby Morrow won gold medals in both events. Morrow was also the anchor man in the 400-meter relay race in which his team finished first. (In the 400-meter relay each man of the four-member team runs 100 meters. At the end of his 100 meters, the runner passes a baton to the next teammate. The anchor man is the last runner on the team.)

Jesse Owens running in the 200-meter race at the 1936 Berlin games

Jesse Owens made Olympic track-and-field history in Berlin in 1936. At that time, Adolf Hitler was the Nazi dictator of Germany. Hitler insisted that blond, blue-eyed people were better than all other people. He said that Jews and blacks had never done anything worthwhile in athletic competition.

61

Hasley Crawford of Trinidad crosses the finish line to win the gold medal for the 100-meter dash in 1976.

Many Germans called the black athletes from America the "Black Auxiliaries."

There were ten blacks on the sixty-six-man American track-and-field team. They listened to the jeers of Hitler's Nazis, smiled, and said nothing. But before the 1936 Olympic games were over, those ten black athletes made Adolf Hitler look foolish.

In the 100-meter race, the winner was Jesse Owens, a black man. Taking second place was Ralph Metcalfe, another black man. Jesse Owens won the 200-meter race. In second place was Mack Robinson, another black man. Mack was the older brother of Jackie Robinson, who became the first black major-league baseball player.

In the 400-meter race, the winner was Archie Williams, a black man. In third place was James LuValle, another black man.

John Woodruff won the 800-meter race. The United States had not won this event in 24 years. Woodruff was a black student attending the University of Pittsburgh.

The high jump was won by Cornelius Johnson, a black American athlete. In second place was Jesse Owens's teammate at Ohio State University, a black athlete named David Albritton.

Fritz Pollard, Jr., whose father had been a great all-American football

62

player at Brown University, took third place in the 100-meter high hurdles. (Hurdles are obstacles that runners jump over. The height of the hurdle is different for different-length races.) Pollard also was black.

The United States won the gold medal in the 400-meter relay. The first leg of the race was run by Jesse Owens. He handed the baton to Ralph Metcalfe.

The broad jump was won by Jesse Owens.

When the games were over, it turned out that America's "Black Auxiliaries" had outscored *every* other national team. These American black athletes had won eight gold medals, three silver medals, and two bronze medals. They had proved once and for all that a champion can have any color skin.

The size of a country doesn't matter either. Smaller nations have produced outstanding teams and athletes: Finland came to the Antwerp Olympics in 1920 with some of the greatest track-and-field stars ever seen.

A Finn named Ville Porhola won the shot-put. (Men use a shot-put weighing 16 pounds. The one for women weighs

The 110-meter hurdle race at the 1976 games

8 pounds 13 ounces.) His teammate, Elmer Niklander, took second place. Niklander won the discus event, and another Finn, Armas Taipale, took second place. Jonni Myyra received a gold medal in the javelin. But the Finns were to win even more medals. Vilho Tuulus was first in the hop-step-jump (this is also called the triple jump). E. R. Lehtonen took first prize in the pentathlon. First place in the marathon was taken by Hannes Kolehmainen, the first of the "Flying Finns." The great Paavo Nurmi finished first in the 10,000-meter run and took second place in the 5,000-meter event.

Shot-put

Steeplechase

Paavo Nurmi was the greatest distance runner of his time. (Long-distance runners run distances of 5,000 meters and over.) He told newspaper reporters that he had trained in his youth by racing a mail train. Often he would beat the train. Nurmi ran with a stopwatch strapped to his wrist. During a race, he would check the stopwatch to see how fast he was running. He was so sure of beating everyone else that he wanted to beat the clock and set new records. He won nine gold medals and three silver medals.

Led by Nurmi, Finland's performance in the 1920 games was amazing. The team from a tiny country won nine gold medals, the same number as the Americans.

In 1924, Finland proved that their success in 1920 was not just luck. At the Paris Olympics, Myyra won the javelin event again. Lehtonen won the pentathlon once more, and 40-year-old Albin Stenroos won the marathon.

Another Finn, Ville "Willie" Ritola, was also outstanding that year. He won the 10,000-meter race and the 3,000-meter steeplechase. (In the steeplechase the runners must jump over barriers, some of which have water behind them.) Ritola also came in second in the 5,000 meters.

But it was Nurmi, as usual, who was

65

Bob Beamon making his record long jump

the star. He won in the 1,500 meters, the 5,000 meters, and the 10,000-meter cross-country race—an event that has since been discontinued. That year the Finns went home with seven gold medals.

The Finns broke many records in 1924, but that was nothing new. New records are set at every Olympic meet. Sometimes records are set in remarkable ways. In 1968, two Americans—Bob Beamon and Dick Fosbury—each broke a record in Mexico City. In both cases the judges and the spectators were amazed.

Bob Beamon came from New York and received his college education at the University of Texas. Beamon was entered in the long jump. The Olympic record in that event—26 feet 7¾ inches—had been set in 1960 by Ralph Boston of the United States. But that was not the world record, only the Olympic record. The world record was 27 feet 4¾ inches. A jump of even 28 feet seemed impossible.

Beamon rocketed down the runway, leaped off on his right foot, and went sailing through the air as if he had been shot out of a cannon. When he landed, the officials could hardly believe their eyes. They measured his jump. Just to make sure, they measured it again.

Beamon had jumped 29 feet 2½ inches. He had broken the world record by almost 2 feet, and the old Olympic record by almost 3 feet! Beamon was so happy that he sank to the ground and cried.

Dick Fosbury became famous because he introduced a brand-new way of doing the high jump. His method is called the "Fosbury Flop" and almost every high jumper uses it now.

Under the old method, a jumper ran up to the bar and took off, facing the bar with the side of his body. He would leap up on his inside foot and "roll" his body over the bar. Usually, the jumper would land in the sawdust on his hands and knees or on his back.

By 1968 the sawdust had been replaced by a large inflated air bag. So the landing was much softer. Fosbury's method might not have worked with sawdust behind the bar. He might have been hurt. But it was fine with the air bag.

Fosbury ran up to the bar and leaped up on his outside foot. At the same time he turned his back to the bar. He went over it headfirst and backward and landed on his shoulder blades.

Fosbury jumped 7 feet 4½ inches to break the Olympic record.

The "Fosbury Flop" came 36 years

Dick Fosbury doing his famous "Fosbury Flop" at the 1968 games too late to help Mildred "Babe" Didrikson. Fosbury would have been disqualified in 1932, because he would not have been allowed to clear the bar headfirst. The rule stated that the bar had to be cleared feetfirst. That rule has now been changed. But that rule was the reason Didrikson lost her third gold medal in 1932.

Babe Didrikson was the greatest all-around woman athlete of her time. Many people say she was the greatest ever. During her career she won many honors. The world first took notice of her in the 1932 Olympics at Los Angeles. But, before that, she had scored some impressive victories.

In July 1932, about two weeks before the start of the Olympics, an amateur track-and-field meet was held at Northwestern University. One of the teams competing was sent by the Employers Casualty Company of Dallas, Texas.

The Texas team won in the shot-put, javelin, broad jump, baseball throw, and 80-meter hurdles. The Texas team also tied for first place in the high jump and placed fourth in the javelin throw. Texas lost out completely in the 100-meter sprint. However, the Texas team won the meet. A team called the Illinois Women's Athletic Club finished second.

The Illinois team consisted of twenty-two girls. The entire Texas team had just one girl—18-year-old Babe Didrikson. She won five events, and tied for first in a sixth.

Babe was allowed to enter only three events at the Olympics. She chose the javelin, the hurdles, and the high jump.

Babe won the javelin and the hurdles. In the high jump, she and her teammate

> Another great jumper was Ray Ewry. He competed in the early Olympics in the standing high jump, standing broad jump, and the standing hop-step-jump. (These events are no longer held.) Ewry won a total of eight gold medals in the Olympic games of 1900, 1904, and 1908.

Mildred Didrikson's friends thought she played baseball so well, they nicknamed her "Babe" after the great Babe Ruth. When some newspaper reporters asked Babe if there was any game she didn't play, she answered, "Dolls."

Babe Didrikson, second from the right, on her way to victory in the 80-meter hurdles at the 1932 Los Angeles games

Jean Shiley were tied at 5 feet 5¼ inches. The judges ordered a jump-off at the same height. Both girls went over the bar, but the judges ruled that Babe had dived over the bar headfirst in her last jump. She insisted she had not, but the judges stood firm. Babe had to settle for the silver medal.

Babe Didrikson was outstanding in any sport she tried. She was named to the women's all-American basketball team three times. Once she pitched in an exhibition game (the game didn't count, it was just for people to watch) for the Philadelphia Athletics, a major-league team. She could play outstanding tennis, and could even box. But it turned out that her best sport was golf. In the late 1940s, she turned professional. She won seventeen golf tournaments in a row. In 1950 she was named the finest female athlete of the previous fifty years. This put Babe in the same company as Jim Thorpe, who was named the finest male athlete of the previous fifty years.

Jim Thorpe, posing in his Olympic uniform at the 1912 Stockholm games

Jim Thorpe was an American Indian. He went to Carlisle College, a school for Indians, where he starred on the baseball, football, and track teams.

Some people said that Jim Thorpe was a one-man track team at Carlisle, but it only seemed that way. In a track meet against undefeated Lafayette College, Thorpe almost did win the meet single-handed. He won the high jump, the shot-put, the discus, the 120-yard high hurdles, and the 220-yard low hurdles. He finished third in the 100-yard dash. There were five other men on the Carlisle team, and they added five more victories to the total.

In the 1912 Olympics at Stockholm, Sweden, Jim Thorpe won the pentathlon and the decathlon. That feat can never be duplicated because the pentathlon is no longer a track-and-field event. He also finished fourth in the high jump.

Jim Thorpe's joy in 1912 was turned to sadness in 1913. The International Olympic Committee discovered that he had once played baseball for money and that made him a professional athlete. Since only amateurs can compete in the Olympics, Thorpe had to return all his medals.

The decathlon is the toughest test of the Olympics. The ten events of the decathlon are held over a period of two days. During the first day, the athlete must compete in the 100-meter sprint, the long jump, the shot-put, the high jump, and the 400-meter race. On the second day, the events are: the 110-meter high hurdles, the discus, the pole vault, the javelin, and the 1,500-meter race.

A decathlon athlete must be an all-around athlete—a sprinter, a middle-distance runner, a jumper, and a thrower. (Middle distances are any distance from 800 meters [2,600 feet] to the 3,000-meter steeplechase [slightly less than 2 miles].)

The contestant need not win every event in the decathlon in order to receive the gold medal. The scoring is done on a point system. Every split second and every half-inch counts, and you don't have to be in first place to get points. The athlete who collects the most points, even if he doesn't win all the events, is the winner.

United States athletes do well in the decathlon. They have won the decathlon nine times from 1912 through 1976. Bob Mathias of Tulare, California, won

The winner of the decathlon is always considered to be the world's greatest all-around athlete.

it twice in a row, in 1948 and 1952. Mathias was only 17 years old when he won the first time. A few months before going to London for the 1948 Olympics, Mathias had never even tried to pole vault and had never held a javelin in his hand. He had been an outstanding athlete at Tulare High School. And his coach, Virgil Jackson, had faith in Mathias.

Bruce Jenner, who won the decathlon in 1976 at Montreal, was another fine athlete who had never tried some of the events before attending college. But Bruce was a natural athlete. He was a champion water-skier. He was a member of the wrestling team when he was in the seventh grade. In high school he played football and was on the track team. Jenner received an athletic scholarship to Graceland, a small college in Iowa, where he began to train as a decathlon athlete. Jenner entered the decathlon event for the first time in the Drake Relays, a college meet. He finished sixth.

But Jenner knew he could do better. The next time he competed in a decathlon, he finished third. Finally, he took first place. The victory made him think he might enter the Olympic trials. It turned out he was good enough to make the team.

At the Munich Olympics in 1972, Jenner finished in tenth place. He was 22 and he knew that he would have only one more chance to compete in the decathlon. He would be too old after 1976.

For the next four years, Jenner did almost nothing but train. His new wife, Chrystie, helped support them with her job as an airline flight attendant.

Jenner knew he had two outstanding rivals for the decathlon championship. One was Nikolai Avilov of Russia. Avilov had won the championship in 1972. The other was Guido Kratschmer of West Germany. There were other fine decathlon athletes entered, but those two seemed to be the best.

Bruce Jenner clears the bar in the pole-vault event of the decathlon.

Bruce Jenner running in a decathlon race

After the five events of the first day, Kratschmer, with 4,333 points, was in the lead. Second was Avilov with 4,315 points. Jenner was third with 4,298 points. These three would fight it out for the gold medal.

After the sixth event, the lead changed hands. Avilov was ahead, Kratschmer dropped to second, and Jenner remained third. Two events later, Jenner was ahead, Kratschmer was still second, but Avilov had fallen to third. The standings were the same after the ninth event. Jenner had 7,904 points, Kratschmer had 7,716, and Avilov had 7,655.

The tenth and final event was the 1,500-meter race. That distance is just

359 feet less than a mile, and is very difficult for the tired athletes. Jenner finished second. It was good enough to give him a total of 8,600 points—a new Olympic decathlon record.

Many things in the Olympics have changed. The standing high jump, tug of war, lacrosse matches, lawn tennis, and the 60-meter dash are some events that have been dropped. Other events are completely different. The pentathlon is one example.

When Jim Thorpe won this event in 1912, it was in the track-and-field category. Thorpe competed in the broad jump, the discus throw, the 200-meter run, the 1,500-meter run, and the javelin. This competition still has five events today, but they are five different events.

The modern pentathlon is a "make-believe" military event in which army personnel compete. The pentathlon takes five days, one day for each event. The event represents the problems a soldier might meet while carrying an important message through enemy territory.

The contestants choose horses by lot. On the first day they ride cross-country for 5,000 meters (3 miles). On the second day the messenger must fence with an épée (ay-PAY) against hostile soldiers who have caught up with him. On the third day, still fighting enemy soldiers, he shoots a pistol at a bobbing target which is 25 meters (75 feet) away.

Ruth Fuchs of East Germany, 1972 and 1976 gold medalist in the women's javelin

America's Alfred Oerter was the only Olympic athlete
to win a gold medal in four consecutive Olympics.
From 1956 through 1968, each time Oerter threw the discus he broke a record.
Naturally, the last three times he *broke his own records.*

On the fourth day the rules assume he has lost his horse, and must swim across a river. So the contestant must swim 300 meters (about 1,000 feet) free style. (Free style means that any stroke can be used. Swimmers today use the front crawl. In the front crawl the swimmer swims face down in the water and uses a flutter kick.) On the final day he must run 4,000 meters (about 2½ miles) to finally deliver the message.

Scoring for the pentathlon is on a point basis, but this scoring is very different from the scoring of the decathlon. In the pentathlon, if a contestant finishes first in an event, he gets one point. The man in second place receives two points, and so on. At the end of the event the man with the *lowest* score wins.

It is the dream of every athlete to be called the best in his or her event—to win a gold medal. Winning two gold medals is a wonderful achievement. Winning three or four in a single Olympics is highly unusual.

In 1972 an American swimmer named Mark Spitz became the greatest swimmer in history. He won *seven* gold medals in one Olympics. Mark Spitz was a swimming champion long before the Munich Olympics. At the age of 18 he competed in the 1968 Olympics in Mexico City. Everyone expected him to win everything in sight, but he didn't live up to their hopes. He won two gold medals, but they were for the relay races—when he was part of a four-man team. He also won a silver medal for the 100-meter butterfly and a bronze medal for the 100-meter free style. (The butterfly stroke has been used since 1952. The swimmer lies face down in the water. Both arms are raised out of the water at the same time while the swimmer also does an up-and-down flutter kick.)

Some of his teammates were happy to see Spitz lose. He was not very popular with them because he was too cocky, too sure of himself.

Mark Spitz, swimming the 200-meter free-style event

Swimmers lined up on starting blocks

Probably his poor showing at Mexico City was the best thing that ever happened to Mark Spitz. He entered Indiana University and became co-captain of the swimming team. He broke twenty-eight world records in the free-style and butterfly events while he was in college.

When the 1972 Olympics came, it was a different Mark Spitz who went to Munich. Spitz was determined to show the world how good he could be.

The first race was the 200-meter butterfly. Spitz knew he could win easily, and he did. He set a new world record, 2 minutes and $7/10$ of a second. Spitz won another gold medal. He was the anchor man in the 400-meter free-style relay. It was another record for the U.S. team.

The next day Spitz added a third gold medal when he won the 200-meter free-style race. He won that race by less than a second. Again he set a record.

Two days later, Spitz added two more gold medals and set two more records. He won the 100-meter butterfly race. Then he was the anchor man in the 800-meter free-style race. The Americans led all the way and they won by 6 seconds.

Now the entire sports world was watching Mark Spitz. Could he win six gold medals? Four athletes before him had won five gold medals in one Olympic meet. In 1904 an American named Anton Heida had won that many in gymnastics. An Italian fencer named Nedo Nadi had won five in 1920. Willis Lee, an American shooter, had won five times in 1920. The great Paavo Nurmi had done it in 1924.

Mark Spitz became the first athlete in Olympic history to win six gold medals in one Olympic game when he finished first in the 100-meter free-style race. He won his seventh gold medal as a member of the 400-meter medley-relay team. Four swimmers, each swimming a different stroke (the backstroke, breaststroke, butterfly, and free style), make up a medley-relay team. In the breaststroke the swimmer's head is out of the water. The swimmer pushes his arms through the water while kicking his legs in a froglike way.

There were other outstanding swimmers in the 1972 Olympics. Roland Matthes of East Germany won two gold medals, in the 100-meter and the 200-meter backstroke. (In the backstroke the swimmer swims on his back and uses one arm at a time to move himself through the water while doing the

In 1896 Alfred Hajos of Hungary won the men's 100-meter free-style swimming event in 1 minute and 22 $\frac{2}{10}$ seconds. Today a man swimming that slowly could not make the team of any nation in the world.

flutter kick.) Matthes had won gold medals in those same events in 1968. Gunnar Larsson of Sweden also took two gold medals, in the 200-meter and the 400-meter individual medley. In the individual medley one swimmer swims a different stroke—the butterfly, backstroke, breaststroke, and freestyle—each time he swims a length or lap of the pool.

In addition, a great favorite of the swimming fans was a 15-year-old blond Australian girl named Shane Gould. Shane won three gold medals: in the 200-meter free style, the 400-meter free style, and the 200-meter individual medley. She took a silver medal in the 800-meter free style and a bronze medal in the 100-meter free style.

The history of the Olympics is filled with stories about athletes or teams that have failed once, but have worked and worked and become winners.

In 1968, Micki King, an American diver, had a very good chance to win in the springboard event. On one of her last dives she had a terrible accident.

Three women swimmers have each won eight Olympic medals. Dawn Fraser of Australia won four gold medals and four silver medals, Shirley Babashoff of the United States won two gold and six silver medals, and Kornelia Ender of East Germany won four gold and four silver medals.

Top: Kornelia Ender of East Germany competing in the 100-meter butterfly event in 1976
Bottom: Shane Gould of Australia, winner of the 200-meter individual medley in 1972

Jennifer Chandler, U.S. winner of the 1976 gold medal for women's springboard diving

Italian Klaus Dibiasi, winner of the men's gold platform diving medal in 1968, 1972, and 1976

She hit the diving board and broke her arm. Although she was in great pain, Micki finished her last dive. But she had lost points due to the accident and finished fourth.

In 1972 Micki was back to try again. This time there were no accidents. She won a gold medal.

In 1956, in Australia, the Yale University rowing crew represented the United States in the eight-oar event. (Racing boats have crews of two, four, or eight oarsmen. Each person holds one oar. In sculling, each person holds two oars. There are one, two, or four scullers. Sometimes a crew member—the coxwain [KOK-son]—steers.) American crews had won this event seven times in a row and it seemed that Yale could do it again. But, in the very first heat, the Americans finished third, losing to Canada and Australia.

The rules for Olympic rowing are different from other events. There is a system called *repêchage* (reh-peh-SHAHZH), which means second chance. Losers in the first round can keep competing, but they must win every race to stay in the event.

Yale's first opponents in the second-chance race were Italy, Great Britain, and France. The Americans won by two lengths. (That means that they were ahead of the second-place team by a distance equal to two lengths of a boat.) They then took on Russia, Japan, and Australia. The Australians had already defeated the Americans once. But not this time. The Americans were first, and the Australians came in second.

Rowers

It had been a difficult race for Yale, but the event wasn't over yet. They still had to face Australia and Canada in the finals. These were the same crews that had beaten the U.S. team in the first heat.

Forty thousand people came to Lake Wendouree, near Melbourne, to watch the 2,000-meter race.

Canada took an early lead, but Australia caught up and nosed in front. The Yale crew was rowing at the rate of thirty-six strokes a minute, which was a little faster than normal for them. At the halfway point they had overtaken the leaders. With about 600 meters to go, Yale increased its strokes to forty per minute. Slowly they edged ahead. It was a close finish. America defeated Canada by a mere half-length. Australia was third.

Captain Tom Charlton declared, "We're the toughest crews ever put together. And we beat the best."

This comment showed the Olympics at its greatest—hard competition and people and teams that respect each other. Sometimes, however, athletes come to the Olympics greatly disliking the athletes from another country. This

Women's quadruple sculls with coxswain

was the case in 1956 when Russia and Hungary faced each other in the water-polo competition. Before the Olympics, Russian tanks and soldiers had invaded Hungary to halt the Hungarian uprising. The athletes remembered this trouble as they got into the pool for the water-polo match.

In water polo, the pool can be between 8 and 20 yards wide, between 20 and 30 yards long, and at least 3 feet deep. Usually the water is deeper. There are seven players on each team. There are nets at each end of the pool. Points are scored by putting the ball into the net.

The ball is moved by dribbling or passing. Dribbling is done with the forearms. Except for the goalkeeper (the player guarding the net), no player may use more than one hand at a time to dribble or pass. The goalkeeper may use two hands, or punch it with his closed fist. Players can swim underwater, but the ball must remain on the surface. There is no body contact with an opponent, unless the opponent has the ball. Ducking an opponent who has the ball is forbidden.

Russia and Hungary had always been strong in water polo. Now these two fine teams were matched against each other. They used their elbows harder than was necessary and there was more contact than the rules allowed. Hungary took a 4–0 lead. With about 2 minutes left to play, it seemed that Hungary would win the game. Then, in going after the ball, Valentin Prokopov of Russia hit Hungary's Ervin Zador just above the eyebrow. Blood flowed from the cut on Zador's eye.

A save in a water-polo match

The game was stopped immediately in order to treat the cut. As the Hungarians glared at them, the Russians decided to leave the pool and forfeit (give up) the game.

But many felt that the Russians were not totally at fault. Wally Wolf, an American water-polo player, had been watching the game and he felt that the Russians had a reason to play rough. He said, "The Hungarians had been pushing Prokopov around all during the game."

Water polo is one of the newer sports played around the world. It is only a little more than a hundred years old. Another new sport is ice hockey. The first hockey game was played in Canada in the 1850s. Basketball is even newer. James Naismith invented basketball in 1891, so that his students at Springfield College, Massachusetts, could play an indoor game. In 1895 a man named William Morgan invented volleyball. Morgan was the physical director at the YMCA in Holyoke, Massachusetts. Volleyball has since become popular throughout the world.

Most other sports began centuries ago. Wrestling, for example, was part of the ancient Olympics. But like all sports, it has changed greatly over the years. In the modern Olympics there are three different kinds of wrestling events: judo, Greco-Roman, and free style.

Judo was first introduced into the Olympic games in 1964. Judo is an old sport. Some forms of judo have been practiced in Asia for hundreds of years.

It is the art of self-defense without weapons.

The Samurai (SAM-ur-eye) warriors of Japan often had to fight with only their hands when they lost their swords or spears in a battle. Later, this fighting skill was developed into *jujitsu* (ju-JIT-su). In jujitsu, the unarmed fighter will poke with his fingers, make chopping motions with his hands, or kick out with his feet. When small handguns were invented, the art of jujitsu began to die out.

Late in the 1800s Dr. Jigoro Kano of Tokyo, began to improve on jujitsu. The result was judo. In judo the important thing is to use the moves of your opponent to get him off balance so that you can throw him.

The Japanese had been early leaders in Olympic competition. But a 6-foot-6-inch, 253-pound Dutchman named Anton Geesink was one of the first to break the hold. Geesink won the gold medal in 1964 in the open weight (no limit) category.

Anton Geesink, at right, Dutch winner of the 1964 gold medal for judo in the open category

In Greco-Roman-style wrestling, wrestlers can grab their opponents above the waist. They may use only their hands and arms. No tripping or tackling is allowed. The wrestler tries to throw his opponent to the mat so that his shoulders are both on the mat at the same time. If the wrestler does this, he scores a fall and the match is over. If he cannot, the match continues for about 20 minutes. If there is no fall at the end of that time, the judges and the referee award the victory on a point system.

Free-style wrestling, super-heavyweight category

In the free style, wrestlers may apply holds below the waist. Tripping and tackling are legal. The wrestler tries to force his opponent's shoulders or head to the mat.

Like boxers, wrestlers are grouped in different weight categories. The lightest wrestlers are called paperweights and the heaviest are super-heavyweights. One of the greatest free-style wrestlers in Olympic history was Alexandr Medved of Russia. In 1964 he won the gold medal as a light heavyweight. In 1968 he won as a heavyweight. In 1972 he took a third medal, this time as a super-heavyweight. Because Medved's weight kept increasing, he was able to compete in three different categories.

Most wrestlers compete in either the free-style or Greco-Roman events, but Wilfried Dietrich of West Germany won both. In 1960 he won the gold medal in both the heavyweight free-style and the heavyweight Greco-Roman-style categories.

Weight lifting, another ancient sport, was first introduced into the Olympics in 1920. There are three kinds of lifts: the military press, the snatch, and the clean-and-jerk.

To do the military press, the weight lifter stands at attention with his toes on a line. Then he bends over, grasps the bar of the weights, and lifts it to his shoulders or neck. The athlete holds the weights in that position for a short time. Then he raises the weights overhead. His legs must not move.

The snatch is done in one movement. There is no stop when the bar gets as high as the neck or shoulders. The lifter must hold the weights overhead while the referee counts 1, 2.

The clean-and-jerk is like the military press. The lifter raises the weights to shoulder or neck level, then lifts them overhead. But he can bend his legs and does not have to keep his toes on a line.

Weight lifters are also grouped by weight. The lightest lifters are flyweights; the heaviest are super-heavyweights. Winners are decided on a point system. Points are awarded according to the total weight lifted.

Vasili Alekseev, Russian super-heavyweight lifter

Weight lifters have been lifting greater and greater weights. Three-hundred-and-thirty-pound super-heavyweight Vasili Alekseev of the U.S.S.R. was the first person to lift a total of 1,322.8 pounds.

Weight lifters always try to lift much more than their own body weight. In the military press and the snatch they can lift between 90 and 125 pounds more than they weigh. In the clean-and-jerk they try to lift more than 180 pounds over their own weight.

Weight lifters eat tremendous quantities of food. At the Olympic cafeteria, a lifter may pile three steaks and a pound of mashed potatoes on his plate. Then he may get back in the line for seconds. But sometimes a weight lifter might want to keep his body weight down. In case of a tie, when two men lift the same weight, the athlete who weighs less is declared the winner. That happened in the 1956 Olympics. Paul Anderson of the United States went on a diet. He ate only one meal a day, a really large meal. Then he went against Humberto Selvetti of Argentina. Both men lifted a total of 1,102 pounds. But Anderson had slimmed down to 304 pounds. Since his rival weighed 316 pounds, Anderson was the winner.

Boxing is another ancient sport. It was first introduced into the Olympics in 1904. There were eight classifications at that time. Today there are eleven weight categories—from light flyweight to heavyweight. The United States won in all eight weights in that first year.

George Foreman, 1968 U.S. gold medalist in the heavyweight boxing division

Muhammad Ali, posing in a gym after his light-heavyweight victory in 1960

America's O. L. Kirk won in two divisions, the bantamweight and the featherweight.

When a boxer wins the gold medal in his division, he usually turns professional. Boxing managers are always eager to sign up the champions. For one great Olympic boxer, though, it was a long wait before he could fight for money.

In 1948 Laszlo Papp of Hungary won the middleweight championship. In 1952 and again in 1956 Papp took gold medals, this time in the light-middleweight category. He wanted to turn professional so that he could earn money from his boxing skills. Hungary, however, usually did not permit any kind of professional athletics. But after Papp had won his third gold medal, Hungary made an exception in the case of this great champion.

In 1957, at the age of 31, Laszlo Papp fought, and won, his first pro fight. In the next six years he won twenty-five boxing matches, and became the undefeated European middleweight champion.

Olympic boxing is different from professional boxing in several ways. In professional fights, a hard punch counts for more than a light tap. In the Olympics, it is not how hard the punch is but how often the punches land that counts. Olympic boxing gloves have a white area marked over the knuckles. Blows can only be struck with that white part of the gloves. All Olympic bouts are scheduled for only three rounds, unlike professional fights which can last for ten or fifteen rounds.

The weigh-in before a fight is very important. It was for a boxer named Pascual Perez of Argentina.

Perez was a flyweight. The upper limit for a flyweight is 112 pounds. When Perez got on the scales, he weighed just a little more than 112 pounds. His teammates tried everything to reduce his weight. They ran around with Perez to sweat off some ounces.

Since 1952 five U.S. boxers who won Olympic gold medals have gone on to win the world's heavyweight championship: middleweight Floyd Patterson (1952); light heavyweight Cassius Clay—now Muhammad Ali (1960); and heavyweights Joe Frazier (1964), George Foreman (1968), and Leon Spinks (1976).

They rubbed his body dry. They even gave him a haircut. But it was no use. Perez was about to be disqualified. He tried to protest but no one would listen. The rules had to be obeyed.

Then someone thought that the scales should be checked. Sure enough, as they had hoped, the scales were wrong. Perez wasn't overweight at all and he went on to win the flyweight championship in the 1948 Olympics. Later, he became the professional flyweight champion of the world.

Another favorite one-on-one (one man against one man or one woman against another woman) competition is fencing. There are three different weapons used in fencing: the foil, the épée, and the saber. The foil looks like a dress sword, except that it is shorter and lighter. It has a blade that bends and a small hand guard. The épée has a triangular blade that does not bend as easily as the foil does. There is a large hand guard at the hilt or handle. The saber has a thin blade that bends. There is a cutting edge all along the front of the blade and on about one-third of the back edge.

No fencing sword has a sharp point or cutting edge. All fencers wear masks, gloves, and protective clothing.

Many of the best fencers come from Europe. Hungarians are masters of the saber. From 1908 through 1964 there were twelve Olympic games. A Hungarian won the gold medal for saber fencing in eleven of them. Dr. Jeno Fuchs won twice in a row, in 1908 and 1912.

Fencing

His countryman Rudolf Karpati did the same thing in 1956 and 1960. For forty-eight years either an Italian or a French fencer won the foil event. Viktor Zhdanovich of the U.S.S.R. won the gold medal in 1960 and broke the Italian and French hold on the event.

Women have been fencing as individuals since 1924 and on teams since 1960. The best teams are from Italy, the U.S.S.R., and Hungary.

Teams from the United States have never done well in fencing. Since fencing has not been an important sport in schools, young people have had no place to learn and train. All schools and schoolyards have basketball courts, though. It seems that all young people in the United States play basketball, so it is no surprise that U.S. basketball teams do so well in the Olympics. Basketball was first introduced to the Olympics as an exhibition event. The rules of basketball have greatly changed since 1904. For example, at one time it was illegal to dribble the ball and then shoot for the basket. The ball had to be passed to another player.

Basketball became a permanent part of the Olympics in 1936. Since that time, U.S. teams have won the gold medal every time except once, when they lost to the Russians.

The final game of the 1972 series was between the United States and Russia. It is a game that people still argue over. With about 10 minutes left in the game, the U.S. team was losing by 10 points. The American team went into a full court press, closely guarding the Russians all over the court. The Russians became confused. The ball changed hands several times, and suddenly the United States was in the lead. Then the Russians were ahead again.

With 30 seconds to go, America's Doug Collins grabbed a loose ball. The United States was behind by a single point. Collins drove for the basket, but he was fouled. He was awarded two foul shots. Collins sank both shots. America took the lead, 50-49. The clock showed

The U.S. basketball team plays the Cuban team at the 1972 games. The U.S. team won the silver medal and the Cuban team won the bronze.

only 3 seconds left to play. Victory for the United States looked certain.

The Russians took the ball out of bounds and tried to pass it to midcourt. An American player hit the ball so that it did not reach the Russians. Everyone thought the game was over and the crowd ran onto the court. But the clock showed that there was still 1 second left to play. The court was cleared and the game continued. The Russians had possession of the ball.

Once again the Russians tried to get the ball in bounds. The pass fell short. It seemed certain that the United States had won. But it wasn't over yet. A British official ruled that the clock had not been set correctly. It had been set at 1 second, but he said it should have been set at 3 seconds. So the clock was pushed back.

The Americans were sure the time had been used up, but the ball was given to the Russians again, and again they tried to pass it into play.

Tom McMillan was guarding the Russian who was trying to pass the ball. McMillan was 6 feet 10 inches tall. He waved his arms and jumped around so that the Russian would not make a good pass. The referee ordered McMillan to back up. Just as McMillan stepped back, the ball was passed. Alexander Belov of Russia leaped high and caught the ball. He came down on his feet and leaped again. He sank the basket.

The Americans protested the game, but it was no use. Russia was declared the winner, 51–50.

Soccer

Field hockey

Just as the Americans have led the field in basketball, the countries of the British Commonwealth have been the stars of field hockey. Britain won in 1908. The sport was dropped from Olympic competition until 1920, when Great Britain won again. The International Olympic committee decided not to hold the field hockey event in 1924. In 1928 and again in 1936 the field-hockey event was held and was won by British-ruled India. Finally, in 1948 field hockey became a regular sport again. India, now no longer ruled by Britain, won in 1948, 1952, and 1956. Pakistan, which had once been part of India, won in 1960. The gold medal was taken by India in 1964. Then it was Pakistan's turn again. At last the winning streak was broken in 1972 when a team from West Germany took the gold medal.

No nation dominates soccer. Maybe that is because soccer is the most popular team sport in the whole world. Every country, large or small, tries to produce a great soccer team. Teams from Great Britain have won three times. Hungary has also won three Olympic titles. Tiny Uruguay, with a population of about three million people, has won twice. The United States has never done well in this sport. But that may change because soccer is growing in popularity in the United States. Some experts say that in a few years a U.S. soccer team may be good enough to win the soccer gold medal.

Equestrian (horse) events have changed greatly since ancient times. There were chariot races in the ancient Olympics. The vehicles often overturned and horses ran wild. But modern horse events are not races. They are exercises to show how well-trained the horses are. The horse will respond to the slightest movement of the rider on its back. In some of the equestrian events, the horse goes through a series of steps. In others, the horse does some exercises in a certain pattern. Jumping over barriers is another part of equestrian events.

The most important equestrian event is the Nation's Cup team-jumping competition. Four riders from each country may enter. Only the top three scores in each of two rounds are counted. There are twelve to fifteen obstacles on a course that is close to 1,000 meters (3/5 of a mile) long. At the Los Angeles games in 1932 none of the competing teams was able to complete the course for the Nation's Cup. So no medals were awarded.

Show jumping

William Steinkraus helped the United States win medals in three Olympic games. In 1952 at Helsinki he was on the show-jumping team that won the bronze medal. He won a gold medal in 1968 for individual show jumping. Twenty years after his first victory, Steinkraus led the U.S. team to a silver medal.

Princess Anne of England, member of the 1976 British equestrian team

At the beginning of the modern Olympics most of the riders were army officers. Riding has become more popular and today most of the riders on the equestrian teams are civilians.

Some Olympic sports are not very well known, but they are just as difficult and rugged as any others. Canoeing has been an Olympic event since 1936. One of the greatest canoers was Gert Fredriksson of Sweden. In 1948, 1952, and 1956 Fredriksson won gold medals in the 1,000-meter kayak (KIGH-yak; a special covered-type of canoe moved with a double-bladed paddle) singles. With teammate Sven Sjodelius, he won the 1,000-meter kayak doubles in 1960.

But that was "flatwater" racing. There were no rapids in the waters. It was just smooth, fast paddling. In 1972 the Olympics added a "white-water"

Slalom course at the 1972 games

slalom race which proved very exciting. The white-water slalom is a very difficult race. The slalom has both the Canadian canoe and kayak categories. It requires great strength, good balance, and excellent timing.

A slalom course can be no longer than 800 meters (not quite half a mile). The water flows swiftly, creating a strong current. There are between twelve and thirty gates along the course. The gates are like doorways that the canoe must go through. A gate is two poles that hang from overhead wires. The poles are only a few feet apart. The gates may be placed in the center of the current or flow of the river. Or, they may be behind rocks. Or, they may even be on the edge of an eddy (a small whirlpool).

To make the race even harder, there are three different kinds of gates. The downstream gate is the simplest of all. The racer just goes through it as fast as possible.

The second kind is the upstream gate. The racer must pass the gate while going downstream. Then he turns his canoe around and paddles upstream through the gate. That is where great strength is important.

Finally, there is the reverse gate. The racer approaches the gate, and then turns the canoe around. He must go through the gate *backward*.

Time is not the only important point in a white-water slalom race. Skill in paddling is even more important than speed. A racer can lose points if he gets careless. If a racer's boat touches one of the poles, the racer loses 10 seconds. If the racer's body touches both poles, the penalty is 20 seconds. If the racer misses the gate and does not go through it, the penalty is 50 seconds.

In 1972 East Germany won first place in all three slalom events—the Canadian singles, Canadian pairs, and kayak singles. The slalom was not held at the 1976 games because of the expense of building the course. But the great popularity of the event may help to bring it back in future competitions.

Yachting is another boat event. Yachting is more popular than many people think. Forty-six nations entered the competitions in the 1960 Olympics and they used 138 boats.

Yachts used in the Olympics are grouped in classes according to their size. The largest cost many thousands of dollars. There are also very simple small boats of 12 feet that are sailed by one person. The boats are grouped by size so that only boats of the same size race against each other.

Seven races are held for each group of boats. Six races count in the scoring. Points are gained according to the order in which the boats finish. The boat that has the highest total number of points wins the event.

The greatest sailor in Olympic history was Paul Elvstrom of Denmark. Elvstrom was only 20 years old when he first competed in 1948. He won the Firefly class. Elvstrom competed in the Finn Monotype class when the Firefly class was dropped. He won gold medals in 1952, 1956, and 1960.

Yachting

Cycling

An Olympic event that almost everyone in the world recognizes and understands is cycling. In many countries, a bicycle is an important way for people to travel. And if the gasoline shortage keeps up, it will become even more popular! People throughout the world learn to ride bicycles when they're very young.

The first Olympic bicycle race took place in 1896 in Athens. The course went from Athens to Marathon and back. The total distance was about 54 miles. At Marathon, the racers had to stop and sign their names on a piece of paper. This showed that they had reached the halfway mark.

The winner of that first race was a Greek named Konstantinidis. He did not have an easy race. First, his bicycle broke down and he had to repair it. Later, he bumped into a carriage. But Konstantinidis kept pedaling away and finally won. He rode the distance in 3 hours, 22 minutes, and 31 seconds. The race is much longer today. The cyclists also pedal much faster. In 1972 the course was 200 kilometers (124 miles), more than twice the distance covered by Kinstantinidis. The winner was Hennie

Kuiper of the Netherlands, with a time of 4 hours, 14 minutes, and 37 seconds.

There are several cycling events in the Olympics. In addition to the road race, there are sprints and even an event for bicycles built for two.

Although volleyball is now an Olympic event, most people from other countries had never seen a volleyball game until World War II. American servicemen and women, on duty overseas, played the game among themselves.

The popularity of volleyball spread quickly. It became an Olympic sport in 1964. Everyone thought the Americans would win, since they had invented the game. But other countries won the first three Olympics. The Japanese women's team played thrilling games against the Russians in 1968 and 1972, and placed second. Finally, in 1976 they won the gold medal.

There are two target sports in the Olympics: one in archery, the other in gun shooting.

Archery

Darrel Pace, 1976 gold medalist for archery

The bow and arrow is one of man's oldest weapons. Yet archery was dropped from the Olympics after 1920. It was not included again until 1972. There were two events that year, one for men and the other for women. Archers shot seventy-two arrows at fixed targets.

The men shot at distances of 30, 50, 70, and 90 meters (97 to 290 feet). Women's distances were 30, 50, 60, and 70 meters. The first-place winners were John Williams and Doreen Wilber, both of the United States. In 1976 the gold medalists were again Americans—Darrel Pace and Luann Ryon.

In gun shooting there are a variety of weapons. The marksmen shoot at targets. Sometimes the targets are still, and other times they move.

In rifle shooting three positions are used: standing, kneeling, and prone (flat on the ground). Each shooter fires twenty bullets in each position, for a total of sixty shots. When using the larger—high-powered—weapons, the distance to the target can range from 200 to 1,000 yards. The smaller weapons—.22 caliber—are limited to 50 meters.

Sport shooters like to aim at moving targets, because that is more of a challenge.

In skeet shooting, clay targets are hurled into the air. They move at a speed of about 30 miles an hour. The targets can be released in high or low flights. Each shooter tries to hit the clay target with a shotgun. Each shooter fires at twenty-four of the round disks, called clay pigeons, then takes an extra shot. Points are awarded for the total number of hits.

The races have been run and all the competitions for the summer Olympics have been held. Records have been broken and medals have been awarded. It is time to go home. But all the athletes will have a chance to say good-by to new friends at the colorful closing ceremony.

105

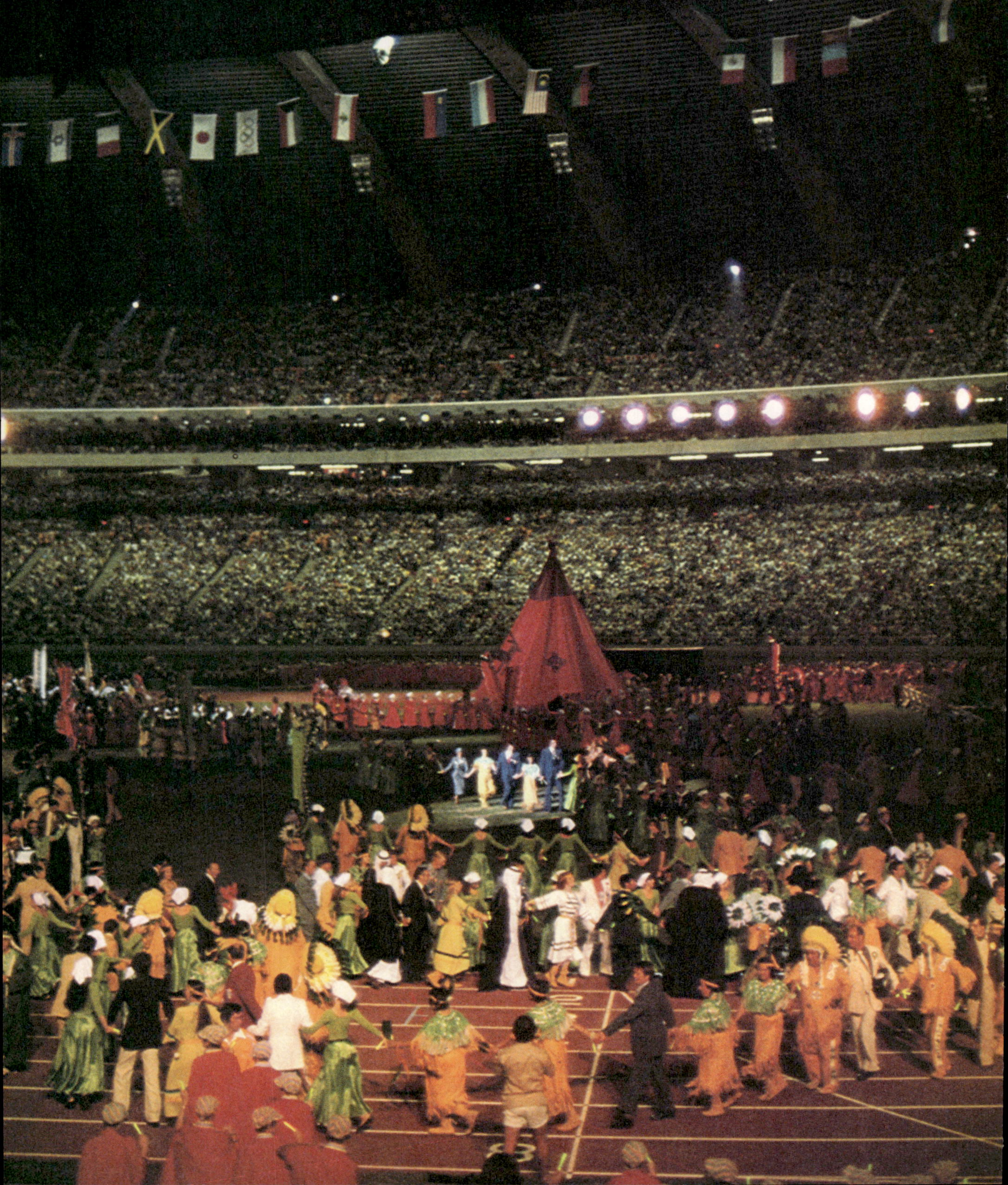

The Closing Olympic Ceremony

After the last event is held and the last medal is awarded, it is time for the ceremony that will end Olympic competition for four years.

At the closing ceremony, the athletes parade into the stadium. A flag bearer and six members of each team march together. All the other athletes mingle in the parade so that all the countries come together for the final day of the Olympics.

The last day of the 1976 games in Montreal was very special. The athletes moved off the track onto the infield during the closing ceremony. Forming a long line, they danced across the field, laughing and singing and shouting. Even some of the spectators came down from the stands to join in the fun.

At the beginning of the games, many of the athletes did not even know their own teammates very well. Even fewer had met the athletes from other countries. But in only two hectic weeks, many of these men and women had become good friends. All the athletes had done their best in the competition and they had come to respect their fellow competitors. Living together in the Olympic village had made strong friendships and good sportsmanship easy.

There are many stories about good sportsmanship at the Olympic games. In 1936 at the Berlin games, Jesse Owens was having a hard time qualifying in the long jump. On his first two

Closing ceremony at 1976 Montreal summer Olympics

tries he fouled by stepping over the line. Luz Long, a German athlete, went over to Jesse Owens and gave him some advice. "I think I know what you are doing wrong," he said. "Why don't you draw a line a few inches in back of the take-off board and jump from there. You'll be sure not to foul."

Owens followed Long's advice, and on his third and final try he did qualify. He then went on to win the event. Luz Long finished second to Owens, and by being so sportsmanlike to a black man he risked angering Adolf Hitler.

Eugenio Monti of Italy was another great Olympian who showed good sportsmanship. He was competing in the two-man bobsled event in the 1964 winter games. He and his teammate had done very well on their runs. The British team had clocked the second fastest time, but broke an axle. After Monti and his teammate had finished their final run of the day, Monti took the axle from his own sled and gave it to the British athletes so that they could continue in the competition that day. The British team was eventually able to win the gold medal the next day. Monti had helped his opponents win, but he went on to win the gold medal in 1968.

For some people, an Olympic gold medal means just a little more because they had to overcome many problems to reach victory. One such person was Wilma Rudolph. Wilma Rudolph was not well as a child. She could not walk properly until she was seven years old.

Athlete at finish line

Friendship at the end of a race

The Olympic flag

But she worked and trained so hard that eventually she could not only walk well, she could run like a deer. She became such a good athlete that she was able to go with the United States Olympic team to Melbourne, Australia, for the 1956 summer games. Wilma won a bronze medal as a member of the 400-meter relay team. She continued to train and work, and she amazed the sports world at the 1960 Olympics in Rome. She became the first American woman to win three gold medals in track events at one game—the 100-meter and 200-meter dashes and the 400-meter relay.

The Olympic flame is put out at the closing ceremony, and then it is time for the athletes to go home. They think about the effort and work required to come to the Olympics, and perhaps the advice that Baron Pierre de Coubertin gave to all Olympic athletes.

"The important thing in these Olympics is not so much winning as taking part. The important thing in life is not the victory but the battle. The essential thing is not to have conquered but to have been a good loser."

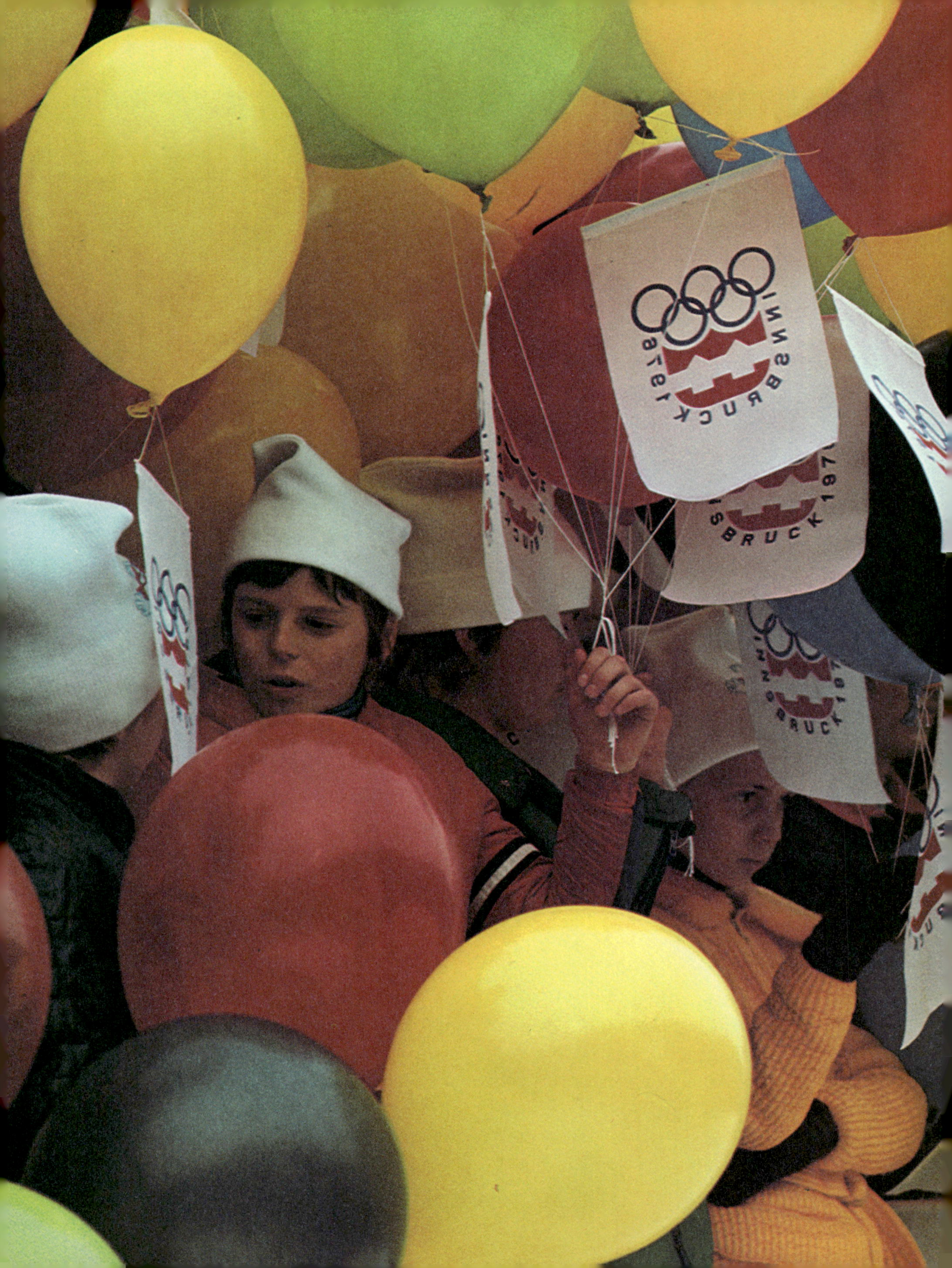
SBRUCK 197

Index

References to pictures are in *italic type*.

A

Albright, Tenley, 51, *51*
Albritton, David, 62
Alekseev, Vasili, *90*
Anderson, Paul, 91
Anne, Princess (Great Britain), *98*
Antwerp *see* Olympics (modern), (1920)
archery, *103*, 103–04
    (1972), 104
    (1976), 104, *104*
Arnette, Jay, 29
Arrachion, 18
Athens:
    Olympics (1896), 22–25, 27, 79, 102
    Olympic-type games (1859), 21
Averoff, George, 22, 25
Avilov, Nikolai, 73, 74
awards:
    ancient Olympics, 15, 16
    modern Olympics, 25, 79

B

Babashoff, Shirley, 81
basketball, 29, 86, 94
    (1960), 29
    (1972), 94–95, *95*
    Russia, 29
    United States, 29, 94
Beamon, Bob, 66, *66*
Bellamy, Walt, 29
Belov, Alexander, 95
Berlin *see* Olympics (modern), (1936)
biathlon, 35
bicycling *see* cycling
Blake, Arthur, 23, 24
boating *see* canoeing; yachting
bobsledding, 35, 42, *43*, 44
    (1932), 42
    (1956), 43
    (1960), 43
    (1964), 43, 108
    (1968), 43, 108
Boozer, Bob, 29
Boston, Ralph, 66
Boston Athletic Club, 23
Bowerman, Bill, 60
boxing, 91, 92
    ancient Olympics, 14, 17
    (1904), 91–92
    (1920), 42
    (1948), 93
    (1952), 92, 93

boxing (*continued*)
    (1956), 92
    (1960), 92, 93
    (1964), 93
    (1968), *91*, 93
    (1976), 93
broad jump (long jump):
    (1896), 24
    (1936), 63
    (1968), 66
Burke, Tom, 23, 24

C

Canada: ice hockey, 45, 46
canoeing, 98–100, *99*
    (1948), 98
    (1952), 98
    (1956), 98
    (1972), 100
ceremony, closing, 105, 107–09, *108*
    (1896), 25
    (1976), *106*, 107
ceremony, opening, 31–33, *33*
    (1896), 23–24
Chamonix *see* Olympics (modern), (1924)
Chandler, Jennifer, *82*
chariot racing (ancient Olympics), 14, 15, 17, 19, 97

Charlton, Tom, 84
Clark, Ellery, 23, 24
Collins, Doug, 94
Comaneci, Nadia, 28, 53–55, *54*, 56
Connolly, James, 23, 24
Constantine, Crown Prince (Greece), 22, 25
Coroebus, 14
Cortina d'Ampezzo *see* Olympics (modern), (1956)
Coubertin, Baron Pierre de, *20*, 21–22, 25, 31
    advice to athletes, 109
Crawford, Hasley, *62*
Curry, John, *50*
Curtis, Tom, 23, 24
cycling, *102*, 102–03
    (1896), 102
    (1972), 102–03

D

Davis, Otis, 60, *60*
decathlon, 71
    (1912), 71
    (1948), 72
    (1952), 72
    (1972), 73
    (1976), *52*, 72, *73*, 73–75, *74*
    United States, 29, 71–75
Dibiasi, Klaus, *82*
Didrikson, Mildred "Babe," 67–69, *69*
Dietrich, Wilfred, 89
Dischinger, Terry, 29
    ancient Olympics, 14, 16
discus:
    (1896), 24
    (1920), 64
    (1956), 76
    (1960), 76
    (1964), 76
    (1968), 76
diving:
    (1968), 80, 82, 83
    (1972), 82, 83
    (1976), *82*

E

Eagan, Eddie, 42
Elvstrom, Paul, 100
end of games *see* ceremony, closing
Ender, Kornelia, 81, *81*
equestrian events *see* chariot racing; riding
Evans, Lee, 61
Ewry, Ray, 68

F

fencing, 93, *93*, 94
   (1908), 93
   (1912), 93
   (1920), 79
   (1956), 94
   (1960), 94
   France, 94
   Hungary, 29, 93, 94
   Italy, 94
      pentathlon, 75
   Russia, 94
field hockey, 96, *96*
   (1908), 96
   (1920), 96
   (1928), 96
   (1936), 96
   (1948), 96
   (1952), 96
   (1956), 96
   (1960), 96
   (1964), 96
   (1972), 96
   Great Britain, 96
figure skating *see* skating, figure
Finland: track and field, 63–66
flag, Olympic, 31, *109*
Fleming, Peggy, *37*
Foreman, George, *91*, 93
Fosbury, Dick, 66–67, *67*, 68
France: fencing, 94

Fraser, Dawn, 81
Frazier, Joe, 93
Fredriksson, Gert, 98
Fuchs, Dr. Jeno, 93
Fuchs, Ruth, *75*

G

Garmisch-Partenkirchen *see* Olympics, (1936)
Garrett, Robert, 22–23, 24, *24*
Geesink, Anton, 87, *87*
George, Prince (Greece), 25
Gould, Shane, 80, *81*
Great Britain: field hockey, 96
Greece: team leads modern Olympic parade, 32
Greek art, ancient, 21
gymnastics, 53–56, *55, 57*
   (1904), 79
   (1956), 55–56
   (1960), 56
   (1964), 56

gymastics (*continued*)
    (1972), 53
    (1976), 28, 53–55, *54*
    Japan, 29

H

Hajos, Alfred, 79
Hamill, Dorothy, *50*
Havlicek, John, 29
Heida, Anton, 79
Heiss, Carol, 51
Helsinki *see* Olympics, (1952)
Henie, Sonja, 36, *36*
Hera, 15
Herakles (Hercules), 13
Herodotus, 15
high jump, 60, 66–67, 68
    (1896), 24
    (1932), 68–69
    (1936), 62
    (1968), 67, *67*
Hitler, Adolf, 61, 62, 108
hockey *see* field hockey; ice hockey
horseback riding *see* riding, horseback
Hoyt, William, 23, 24, *24*
Hungary: fencing, 29, 93, 94
hurdles, 63
    (1896), 24
    (1932), 68, *69*
    (1936), 62–63
    (1976), *63*

I

ice hockey, 29, 35, 45, *45*, 86
    (1920), 45, 46
    (1924), 46
    (1928), 46
    (1932), 46
    (1936), 45
    (1948), 45, 46
    (1952), 45, 46
    (1956), 45
    (1960), 46–47
    (1964), 47
    (1968), 47
    (1972), 47
    Canada, 45, 46
    Russia, 29, 45, 46, 47
Imhoff, Darrall, 29
Innsbruck *see* Olympics, (1964); Olympics, (1976)
International Olympic Committee, 31, 35, 71, 96
Italy: fencing, 94

J

Jackson, Virgil, 72
Jamison, Herbert, 23
Japan: gymnastics, 29
javelin, *75*
    ancient Olympics, 14, 16
    (1920), 64
    (1924), 65

(1932), 68
(1952), 59
(1972), 75
(1976), 75
Jenner, Bruce, *52*, 72–75, *73, 74*
Jenner, Chrystie, 73
Johnson, Cornelius, 62
judo, 86–87
(1964), 87, *87*
jujitsu, 87
jumping (horseback riding) *see* riding, horseback
jumping (skiing) *see* ski jumping
jumping (track and field):
   ancient Olympics, 14, 16
   modern Olympics *see* broad jump (long jump); high jump; triple jump

K

Kano, Dr. Jigoro, 87
Karpati, Rudolf, 94
Kaufmann, Carl, 60
kayak *see* canoeing
Killy, Jean-Claude, 40, *41*
King, Micki, 80, 83
Kirk, O. L., 92
Kolehmainen, Hannes, 64
Konstantinidis (bicycler), 102
Korbut, Olga, 53, 55, *55*
Kratschmer, Guido, 73, 74
Kuiper, Hennie, 102–03

L

Lake Placid *see* Olympics, (1932); Olympics, (1980)
Lane, Francis, 23
Larsson, Gunnar, 80
Latynina, Larissa, 55–56
Lee, Willis, 79
Lehtonen, E. R., 64, 65
London *see* Olympics, (1908)
Long, Luz, 108
long jump (broad jump):
   (1896), 24
   (1936), 63
   (1968), 66
Los Angeles *see* Olympics, (1932)
Loues, Spiridon, 25, *25*
Lucas, Jerry, 29
luge *see* tobogganing
LuValle, James, 62

M

McMillan, Tom, 95
marathon:
   (1896), 25
   (1920), 64
   (1924), 65
   (1952), 59
Mathias, Bob, 71–72
Matthes, Roland, 79, 80
Medved, Alexandr, 89
Melbourne *see* Olympics, (1956)
Metcalfe, Ralph, 62, 63
Mexico City *see* Olympics, (1968)
Meyer, Debbie, 28–29
Mittermaier, Rosi, *38, 39*
Molterer, Anderl, 39
Monti, Eugenio, 43, 108
Montreal *see* Olympics, (1976)
Morgan, William, 86

Morrow, Bobby, 61
motto, Olympic, 19
Muhammad Ali (Cassius Clay), *92*, 93
Munich *see* Olympics, (1972)
Myyra, Jonni, 64, 65

N

Nadi, Nedo, 79
Naismith, James, 86
Nero, 19
newspaper and magazine coverage, 27, 28
Niklander, Elmer, 64
Nurmi, Paavo, 64–65, 65–66, 79

O

oath, Olympic, 32
Oerter, Alfred, 76
Olympia (valley, Greece):
    archway, *12*
    temples, building and game sites, 14, 15, *18*, 21
        Heraeum, 15
        Olympium (temple of Zeus), 15, 21
    torch lit for modern games every four years, 31
olympiad, 14
Olympics (ancient), 13–19
    awards of olive wreaths, 15
        winners become heroes, 16
    ending of, in A.D. 394, 19
    events, 14–18, 86, 97
    legends and stories about, 18, 19, 21
    lighting the flame at altar of Zeus, 14
    training for, 16
Olympics (modern):
    (1896), 22–25, 27, 79, 102
    (1900), 68
    (1904), 68, 79, 91–92
    (1908), 35, 68, 93, 96
    (1912), *70*, 71, 75, 93
    (1920), 35, 42, 45, 46, 63–64, 65, 79, 96
    (1924), 35, 36, 46, 65–66
    (1928), 36, 46, 96
    (1932), 36, 42, 46, 61, 68–69, *69*, 97
    (1936), 36, 45, *61*, 61–63, 96, 107–08
    (1948), 38, 45, 46, 59, 61, 72, 93, 96, 98, 100
    (1952), 45, 46, 51, 59, 61, 72, 92, 93, 96, 98, 100
    (1956), 32, 38–40, 43, 45, 51, 55–56, 61, 76, 83–84, 85–86, 91, 92, 94, 96, 98, 100, 109
    (1960), 29, 43, 46–47, 49, 51, 56, 60, 61, 76, 89, 92, 93, 94, 96, 98, 100
    (1964), 43, 47, 49, 56, 61, 76, 87, *87*, 89, 93, 96, 108
    (1968), 28–29, *37*, 40, *41*, 43, 47, 60, 61, *66*, 66–67, *67*, 76, 77, 78, 80, 82, 83, 89, *91*, 93, 98, 103, 108
    (1972), *37*, 47, 53, 73, 75–80, *81*, 82, 83, 89, 94–95, *95*, 96, 98, 100, 102–03, 104
    (1976), 26, *26*, 28, 30, 32–33, *33*, *38*, *39*, *47*, *50*, *52*, 53–55, *54*, 56, *62*, *63*, 72, *73*, 73–75, *74*, *81*, *82*, 93, *98*, 103, 104, *104*, *106*, 107
    (1980), 28
    awards of medals, 25
        winners of five or more gold medals, 79
    beginning of, 22
    choosing of athletes, 29
    closing ceremony, 105, 107–09, *108*
        (1896), 25
        (1976), *106*, 107
    events, changes in, 68, 71, 75
    feeding and housing of athletes, 27, 28
    flag, 31, *109*
    health of athletes, 27
    money for, 22, 27
    motto, 19
    newspaper, magazine, and television coverage, 27, 28
    oath, 32
    opening ceremony, 31–33, *33*
        (1896), 23–24
    preparations for, 27–28
    records, 66
    summer, 28, 53–105
    symbol of five rings, 14, 31

tickets to, 28
tourists, 28
training for, 28–29, 58
winter, 28, 35–51
    sports not in early modern Olympics, 27, 35
Oslo *see* Olympics (modern), (1952)
Owens, Jesse, 61, *61*, 62, 63, 107–08

P

Pace, Darrel, 104, *104*
Paine, John, 23, 24
Paine, Summer, 23, 24
pancratium (ancient Olympic event), 17–19
Papp, Laszlo, 92
Paris *see* Olympics (modern), (1924)
Patterson, Floyd, 93
pentathlon:
    ancient Olympics, 16
    (1912), 71, 75
    (1920), 64
    (1924), 65
    modern Olympics, 71, 75–76
Perez, Pascual, 92–93
Peters, Jim, 59
Pherenice, 16
Phidias, 15
Pindar, 15, 21
Pisidores, 16
pole vault, 23, *73*
    (1896), 24

Pollard, Fritz, Jr., 62–63
Porhola, Ville, 63
postage stamps, Olympic, 22
Poulydamus, 18
Prokopov, Valentin, 85, 86

R

riding, horseback, 97–98, *97*
    (1932), 97
    (1952), 98
    (1968), 98
    (1976), *98*
    in pentathlon, 75
Ritola, Ville "Willie," 65.
Robertson, Oscar, 29
Robinson, Jackie, 62
Robinson, Mack, 62
Rodnina, Irina, *37*
Roman art, ancient, 21
Rome *see* Olympics (modern), (1960)
rowing, 83, *83*, *84*
    (1956), 83–84
    sculling, 83
    United States, 83
Rudolph, Wilma, 108–09
running:
    ancient Olympics, 14, 15, 16
    modern Olympics *see* decathlon; marathon; pentathlon; track and field, hurdles, running, sprints, and steeplechase
Russia:
    basketball, 29
    fencing, 94
    ice hockey, 29, 45, 46, 47
    weight lifting, 29
Ryon, Luann, 104

S

Sailer, Anton, 38–40
sculling *see* rowing
Selvetti, Humberto, 91

Shiley, Jean, 68–69
shooting, 103, 104–05
   (1896), 24
   (1920), 79
   in biathlon, 35
   in pentathlon, 75
   rifle, 105
   skeet, 105
shot-put, 23, 63–64, *64*
   (1896), 24
   (1920), 63, 64
Sjodelius, Sven, 98
skating, figure, 35, *36*
   (1924), 36
   (1928), 36
   (1932), 36
   (1936), 36
   (1952), 51
   (1956), 51
   (1960), 51
   (1968), *37*
   (1972), *37*
   (1976), *50*
skating, speed, 35, 47, *48*, 49, *49*
   (1960), 49
   (1964), 49
   (1976), 47
skiing:
   in biathlon, 35
   cross-country, 35, 42, *42*
   downhill, 35, 38
     (1956), 39–40
     (1968), 40, *41*
     (1976), *39*
   slalom, *34*, 35, 38
     (1956), 39
     (1968), 40
     (1976), *38*
ski jumping, 35, 40, *40*, 47
Skoblikova, Lidija, 49, *49*
sledding *see* tobogganing
Sloane, William Milligan, 22–23
soccer, 96, *96*
Socrates, 15
Sologubov, Nikolai, 46–47

speed skating *see* skating, speed
Spinks, Leon, 93
Spitz, Mark, 76–79, *77*
Squaw Valley *see* Olympics, (1960)
Start of games *see* ceremony, opening
steeplechase, 65, *65*
   (1924), 65
Steinkraus, William, 98
Stenroos, Albin, 65
Stockholm *see* Olympics (modern), (1912)
summer Olympics, 28, 53–105
   see also specific years under Olympics swimming, 76, *78*
   (1896), 24–25, 79
   (1968), 28–29, 78, 80
   (1972), 76–80, *81*
   (1976), *81*
   backstroke, 79–80
   breaststroke, 79
   butterfly, 77, *81*
   free style, 76, *77*, *81*
   medley, 79, 80
   in pentathlon, 76
   see also diving
symbol, Olympic, 14, 31

T

Taipale, Armas, 64
television coverage, 28
Theagenes, 19
Theodosius I, 19
Thorpe, Jim, 69, *70*, 71, 75
tobogganing, 35, 42, *45*
Tolan, Eddie, 61
track and field:
    ancient Olympics, 14, 15, 16
    broad jump (long jump):
        (1896), 24
        (1936), 63
        (1968), 66
    discus:
        (1896), 24
        (1920), 64
        (1956), 76
        (1960), 76
        (1964), 76
        (1968), 76
    Finland, 63–66
    high jump, 60, 66–67, 68
        (1896), 24
        (1932), 68–69
        (1936), 62
        (1968), 67, *67*
    hurdles, 63
        (1896), 24
        (1932), 68, *69*
        (1936), 62–63
        (1976), *63*
    javelin, *75*
        (1920), 64
        (1924), 65
        (1932), 68
        (1952), 59
        (1972), 75
        (1976), 75
    modern Olympics, changes in events, 68, 71, 75
    pole vault, 23, *73*
        (1896), 24
    running, middle-distance and long-distance, 65, 71
        (1920), 64
        (1924), 65–66
        (1936), 62
        (1948), 59
        (1952), 59
        relay, 61
    shot-put, 23, 63–64, *64*
        (1896), 24
        (1920), 63, 64
    sprints, 23
        (1896), 24
        (1932), 61
        (1936), 61, *61*, 62, 63
        (1948), 61
        (1952), 61
        (1956), 61, 109
        (1960), 60
        (1968), 60
        (1976), *62*, *63*

track and field (*continued*)
  steeplechase, 65, *65*
    (1924), 65
  triple jump, 24
    (1896), 24
    (1920), 64
    United States, 29, 61
  see also decathlon; pentathlon
triple jump, 24
  (1896), 24
  (1920), 64
Tuulus, Vilho, 64
Tyler, Albert, 23

U

Ulanov, Alexei, *37*
United States:
  basketball, 29, 94
  decathlon, 29, 71–75
  modern Olympics, resuming of, 22–25
  rowing, 83
  track and field, 29, 61

V

volleyball, 86, 103
  (1968), 103
  (1972), 103
  (1976), 103

W

water polo, 85, 86, *86*
  (1956), 85–86
weight lifting, 89, *90*, 91
  (1956), 91
  Russia, 29
West, Jerry, 29
Wilber, Doreen, 104
Williams, Gardner, 23, 24–25
Williams, John, 104

winter Olympics, 28, 35–51
  sports not in early modern Olympics, 27, 35
  see also specific years under Olympics (modern)
Wolf, Wally, 86
women:
  and ancient Olympics, 15–16, 17
  and early modern Olympics, 27
Woodruff, John, 62
wrestling:
  ancient Olympics, 14, 16–17, 86
  free style, 86, *88*, 89
    (1960), 89
    (1964), 89
    (1968), 89
    (1972), 89
  Greco-Roman, 86, 88, 89
    (1960), 89
  judo, 86–87
    (1964), 87, *87*

Y

yachting, 100, *101*
  (1948), 100
  (1952), 100
  (1956), 100
  (1960), 100
Yale University rowing crew, 83–84
Young, Sheila, *47*

Z

Zador, Ervin, 85
Zappas, Evgenios, 21
Zatopek, Dana, 59
Zatopek, Emil, *58*, 58–60
Zeus, 13, 14
  altar of, 14
  coin of, 15
  statue of, by Phidias, *15*
  temple of (Olympium), 15, 21
Zhdanovich, Viktor, 94

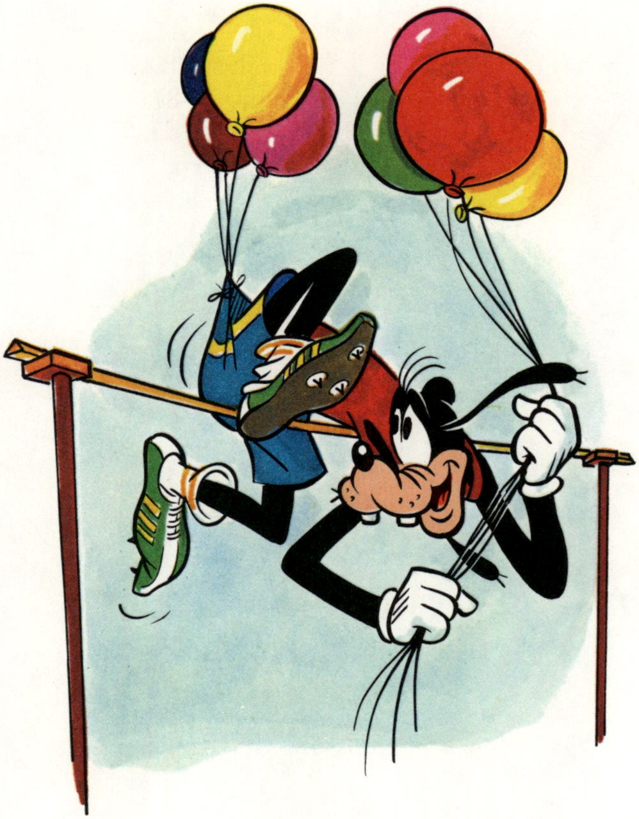